Quick

This g  re shown
together. manner: following

WATERFOWL ,   , Swans, Ducks)

UPLAND GAME BIRDS (Partridge, Grouse, Turkey, Quail) – LOONS –
GREBES – PELICAN – CORMORANT – WADING BIRDS (Bittern, Herons, Egrets,
Ibis)

VULTURE – DIURNAL RAPTORS (Eagles, Hawks, Falcons)

RAILS - COOT – CRANE - SHOREBIRDS (Plovers, Stilt, Avocet, Sandpipers,
Dowitcher, Snipe, Phalaropes)

GULLS - TERNS – PIGEON – DOVES

OWLS – NIGHTHAWK – POORWILL – SWIFTS – HUMMINGBIRDS – KINGFISHER

WOODPECKERS – FLYCATCHERS (Wood-Pewee, Flycatchers, Phoebe,
Kingbirds)

SHRIKES – VIREOS – CORVIDS (Jays, Nutcracker, Magpie, Crow, Raven) –
LARK – SWALLOWS

CHICKADEES – TITMOUSE – BUSHTIT – NUTHATCHES – CREEPER - WRENS –
DIPPER –KINGLETS – GNATCATCHER – THRUSHES

CATBIRD – THRASHER – STARLING – PIPIT – WAXWINGS – WARBLERS –TANAGER

NATIVE SPARROWS AND BUNTING (Towhees, Sparrows, Junco, Longspur,
Grosbeaks, Bunting)

BLACKBIRDS (Blackbirds, Meadowlark, Grackle, Cowbird, Oriole) –
FINCHES (Finches, Crossbills, Siskin) – HOUSE SPARROW

BIRDS OF
INLAND NORTHWEST
AND NORTHERN ROCKIES

By

Harry Nehls
Mike Denny
Dave Trochlell

R.W. Morse Company
Olympia, Washington

For Jeff Nehls (HN)

For Merry Lynn,
my friend, wife, and birding companion (MD)

For Craig Roberts (DT)

Published by the R.W. Morse Company, Olympia, Washington
Copyright ©2008 by the R.W. Morse Company

Library of Congress Control Number: 2008925505
ISBN 9780964081062   **$18.95 Softcover**
First Edition 2008

Printed by
Mantec Production Company, Hong Kong

Authors
Harry Nehls, Mike Denny, Dave Trochlell

Editors
Cathy and Dave Trochlell

Cover and Interior Design
Gina Calle, Ecuador

Map
Shawn K. Morse

Bird Drawings
Eric Kraig

Front Cover Photograph of Osprey
Peter Stahl

Contents

Map of Inland Northwest
and Northern Rockies .... inside front cover

Quick Guide to Local Birds .... inside front cover

Common Local Birds vii

Introduction 1

Identifying Birds 3

Attracting Birds to Your Yard 7

Bird Habitats in the Inland Northwest & Northern Rockies 11

Birding in the Inland Northwest & Northern Rockies 13

Helpful Resources 14

Species Accounts 16

Acknowledgments, Photographer Credits 415

Index/Checklist 417

About the Authors 422

Short Index to Species .... inside back cover

Common Local Birds

Here are some of the most common birds in the Inland Northwest and Northern Rockies. For more information about each bird, go to its Species Account.

Mallard
pg. 30

Female

Male

Great Blue Heron
pg. 86

California Quail
pg. 68

Red-tailed Hawk
pg. 108

Adult

Juvenile

American Kestrel
pg. 114

American Coot
pg. 120

Canada Goose
pg. 22

American Crow
pg. 256

Common Nighthawk
pg. 194

Killdeer
pg. 126

Rock Pigeon
pg. 166

Common Raven
pg. 258

Northern Flicker
pg. 220

Male

Western Kingbird
pg. 236

Black-billed Magpie
pg. 254

Mourning Dove
pg. 168

House Wren
pg. 290

Barn Swallow
pg. 272

European Starling
pg. 318

Cliff Swallow
pg. 270

Mountain Chickadee
pg. 276

Black-capped Chickadee
pg. 274

American Robin
pg. 310

White-crowned Sparrow
pg. 370

Cedar Waxwing
pg. 322

ix

Red-winged Blackbird
pg.384

Female

Male

Brewer's Blackbird
pg.390

Western Meadowlark
pg.386

House Finch
pg.402

Female

Bullock's Oriole
pg.394

Male

Dark-eyed Junco
pg.374

House Sparrow
pg.412

American Goldfinch
pg.408

x

Introduction

Bird watching, or birding, has become one of America's most popular outdoor activities. It is estimated that one-fifth of all Americans – 46 million people – either watch or feed birds. Birding can be great family entertainment. It is easy to get started, inexpensive, improves your observation skills, and allows us to understand and appreciate the natural world and the careful stewardship it requires.

Given the popularity of bird watching and the wide array of habitats and birds in the Inland Northwest and Northern Rockies, it is little wonder that the people in this area enjoy seeing and learning about local birds. The region has a rich variety of bird life with over 260 species of birds that are permanent residents or regular annual visitors. These are the birds featured in this guide.

Birds of the Inland Northwest and Northern Rockies is for beginning bird watchers who wish to identify the birds in our part of the country. This guide will also appeal to experienced birders who wish to learn more about the behavior, habitats, and seasonal occurrence of our local birds, and enjoy their spectacular photographs.

GEOGRAPHICAL COVERAGE

Birds of the Inland Northwest and Northern Rockies includes Eastern Oregon, Eastern Washington, all of Idaho, and Western Montana. This encompasses the area east of the Cascade Mountains in Oregon and Washington, across Idaho and through the Rocky Mountains of Montana. The entire geographical area is depicted on the map inside the front cover.

CONSERVATION

Diverse and thriving bird life is an excellent indicator of a healthy environment. Although the Inland Northwest and Northern Rockies has not seen the degree of development experienced in the Puget Sound and Willamette Valley areas, there has been rapid development around our larger cities. With this development and sprawl

1

comes the clearing of trees and other native vegetation which means the loss of vital habitat that our native birds require for survival. Bird conservation is important, because native birds are the masters of insect control, dead animal scavenging, plant pollination, and seed dispersal.

Those who enjoy birds and wish to protect them should do all they can to protect the birds and their natural habitats. We urge you to join and become active in one or more of the many conservation organizations such as American Bird Conservancy, Ducks Unlimited, Sierra Club, The Nature Conservancy, The Wilderness Society, and other local and regional organizations such as Hells Canyon Preservation Council, Idaho Conservation League, Montana Conservation Science Institute, Oregon Field Ornithologists, Oregon Wild, and Washington Ornithological Society.

There are over a dozen local National Audubon Society chapters and a number of local bird clubs that strive to educate people, and address and improve environmental conditions that impact birds and subsequently mankind. The chapters and bird clubs are located in:

Eastern Oregon: Bend, John Day, Klamath Falls, La Grande
Eastern Washington: Ellensburg, Moses Lake, Spokane, Tri-Cities, Walla Walla, Wenatchee, Yakima.
Idaho: Boise, Coeur d'Alene, Idaho Falls, Moscow, Pocatello, Twin Falls
Western Montana: Bozeman, Dillon, Hamilton, Helena, Kalispell, Missoula, Polson

Identifying Birds

At first, the process of learning to identify birds may seem confusing and difficult. Many birds are very small, move quickly, remain hidden in dense cover, and can look very similar to other birds. First, look at the general shape, size, and color of the bird. Check the Common Local Birds (pages vii - x) and see if it is there. If not, scan through the Species Account pages. Read the description—especially the boldfaced text—to see how it matches your bird. Compare range, similar species, voice, and habitat. Keep comparing until you have a match.

The colors and patterns of a bird's feathering ("plumage") and bare parts (bill, legs, feet, eyes) provide some of the best clues to identify a bird. Beware, however, that plumages may vary within the same species between the sexes, between adults and younger birds, by season, and by geographical location. Learn the parts of a bird; consult the diagrams on pages 4 and 5. Often birds can be identified by head pattern alone.

Good examples of birds where the male and the female have distinctly different plumages are Mallard, House Finch, and Red-winged Blackbird. Usually males have more brilliant colors, as in these examples, while females have muted colors. Other species such as Rock Pigeon, Black-billed Magpie, American Crow, and Western Meadowlark show no plumage differences between the sexes.

Most birds seen in our area in spring and summer display what is known as their breeding (or "summer") plumage. Birds seen here in winter are usually in their non-breeding (or "winter") plumage. Often the breeding plumage is more colorful or highly patterned than the non-breeding plumage.

Most birds display different plumages as they mature. Some birds, such as gulls, require up to four years to attain adult plumage.

The term "juvenal plumage" refers to the first true plumage worn

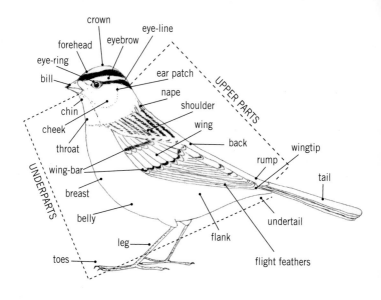

crown
eye-line
forehead
eyebrow
eye-ring
bill
ear patch
UPPER PARTS
chin
nape
cheek
shoulder
throat
wing
wing-bar
back
wingtip
rump
tail
breast
belly
UNDERPARTS
leg
flank
undertail
toes
flight feathers

Parts of a Bird. It is helpful to know the names of the different parts of a bird. These sketches of a White-crowned Sparrow and a Mallard in flight show the terms used to describe bird anatomy in this guide.

by a young bird (a "juvenile") after it molts its downy feathers. Some species maintain this plumage for only a few weeks after fledging while others may hold it into winter. "First-year plumage" refers to the plumage held during the first 12 months of a bird's life. "Immature" refers to all plumages before the bird gains its adult plumage. For many species, immature males may closely resemble females.

Plumage colors and patterning may vary considerably among birds of the same species across geographical populations. For instance, the dark rusty brown Song Sparrow of the northern Columbia

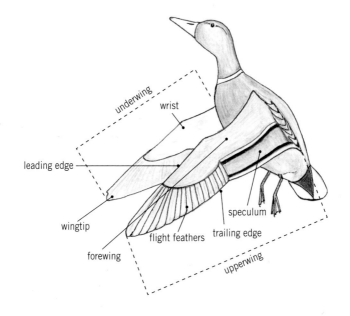

underwing

wrist

leading edge

wingtip

forewing

flight feathers

speculum

trailing edge

upperwing

Basin, Idaho, and western Montana looks different from the pale-breasted, fine-streaked Song Sparrow of the central and southern Blue Mountains and northern Great Basin.

Differences within a species can be great even within the same local population; for example, the majority of Red-tailed Hawks in our area have light breasts and underwings, yet a certain percentage have dark brown to blackish underparts and underwings with lighter-colored flight feathers. Such consistently different types are called "color morphs" (or just "morphs").

Don't expect every bird you see to look exactly like the photographs in this guide. Like people, birds are individuals. To appreciate how variable birds of the same species can be study the ones that come regularly to your backyard feeder. Male House Finches, for

5

example, can show a wide range of coloration from rich, deep red to golden yellow. You may find that, with practice, you can learn to recognize individual birds by the subtle differences in their markings.

In this book the birds are presented in family groupings, as shown in the Quick Guide to Local Birds (inside the front cover). Learning the characteristics of the different bird families will make bird identification easier, quicker, and less stressful. Birds in the same family tend to show similarities in appearance and behavior. A bird's structure, including head shape, general body shape, and length of its wings, tail, legs, and bill, provide important clues to both the family to which it belongs and, often, its species.

Although we have focused on colors, patterns and shapes, the field identification of birds is greatly enhanced by observing behaviors and vocalizations that are unique to a species. Experienced birders can recognize virtually all of the area's species by their calls and songs alone. Be sure to use the section on Voice to arrive at your identifications, and pay close attention in the field to the sounds that birds make.

Attracting Birds to Your Yard

Most people get involved in bird watching by observing the birds that appear in their yards. Perhaps the easiest way to see birds is to put up feeders and watch for birds to appear. When they are perched and eating, birds tend to stay long enough for you to study the field marks at close range and identify them.

Although just hanging out a birdseed feeder will attract some birds, a complete backyard bird program has four important requirements: food, water, cover, and proper hygiene. With careful attention to all four of these elements you will not only increase the number and variety of birds that visit your yard, but you will also be contributing to their well-being. Many helpful books and brochures on bird feeding, nest boxes, and gardening for wildlife are available at nurseries as well as nature and feed stores.

FOOD

The food that birds eat comes mainly from natural sources. Native and ornamental shrubs, trees, and other plants provide fruits, seeds, flowers, and insects. You will attract more birds to your yard by selecting plants favorable to birds. Nearby habitat also provides important protection of the birds from predators.

You may also provide seed, suet, and other products to entice birds to your yard. Many seeds are suitable for feeding birds, although the best product in our area is black-oil sunflower seed, which has high fat content. Another popular winter bird food is niger thistle seed. Many grocery and hardware stores sell a birdseed mix that contains some black-oil sunflower seed but often has a lot of filler grains such as milo, safflower, and weed seeds. When you place this seed in a hanging feeder some of the birds will eat only the sunflower seed and kick the poor-quality filler seeds to the ground. In elevated feeders, it is much better to use only black-oil sunflower seed or a specialized mix of seed that is high in nutritional value.

Different birds have different feeding preferences. You may wish to try more than one of the following common feeder types, depending on the species of birds you wish to attract.

- **Fly-through and hopper feeders** are hung or mounted on a pole or deck, normally five to six feet above the ground. Stocked with black-oil sunflower seed, they may attract chickadees, finches, and other species. If placed properly, such feeders will discourage squirrels (the introduced Eastern Fox Squirrel is a notorious feeder destroyer and raider in much of our area).

- A **ground feeder or platform feeder** is placed near the ground or up to table height and filled with millet, corn, or a birdseed mix that has some black-oil sunflower seeds but is mostly millet. This feeder will attract doves, pigeons, towhees, various sparrows, and juncos. Buy a ground feeder with a bottom screen that allows the rain to drain through to avoid feeding moldy or wet seed to the birds.

- **Cylindrical tube feeders** are either hung or mounted and can be filled with a nutritional mix of birdseed or just black-oil sunflower seed. They attract the smaller birds such as chickadees and finches.

- A specialized tube feeder or sock to hold niger thistle seed is called a **thistle** or **finch feeder** and can attract numbers of goldfinches and, in some years, Pine Siskins.

- **Suet** cakes purchased from a nature or feed store attract woodpeckers, nuthatches, wrens, chickadees, and a host of other birds seeking high-energy fat. Pure beef suet is also attractive, but should only be used during the coldest months.

- **Red hummingbird feeders** attract hummingbirds. It is easy to make hummingbird nectar: mix one part sugar to four parts water, boil, let cool, and then fill your feeders. Do not add any artificial food coloring; it can harm the hummingbirds and the red of the feeder is sufficient to attract them. Never use honey as a sweetener in hummingbird feeders. Bullock's Orioles and House Finches may take sugar water from these feeders as well (orioles also like oranges cut in half and placed around the yard). Place several humming-bird feeders at well-separated sites to discourage a single aggressive hummer from excluding all others. Change the solution in the feeder every few days or sooner if it becomes cloudy.

Experiment with your feeder locations and different bird seed to learn what works best in your yard. Feeders should be placed close to natural shelters such as bushes and trees so the birds can escape from predators. You can feed the birds all year long without worrying that your bird feeding will delay the birds' migration. They will leave when the time is right.

WATER

Birds need water for bathing and drinking. You will find that you attract more birds if you offer a reliable source of clean water in your yard. Consider placing a concrete birdbath filled with one inch of water to meet their needs. Be sure the bottom surface is rough, so that the birds can get a good footing. Place the birdbath near shrubs or trees where birds can preen after bathing and escape from predators. Try adding a dripper to the birdbath. The sound of dripping or running water attracts birds. Water is even more important in the winter and can be kept ice-free with an inexpensive water heater. Remember to keep the water clean and refresh it daily.

COVER AND NEST BOXES

Birds need cover for shade and protection from inclement weather and predators. Nearby bushes, shrubs, and trees will help meet their needs as will a loosely stacked brush pile. Neighborhood cats can be a real problem, especially when they lurk beneath feeders and birdbaths. You can help protect birds by carefully locating or screening off feeders and birdbaths, or by placing chicken wire strategically in front of favorite cat-stalking areas. Keep your cats indoors and encourage your friends and neighbors to do the same.

Some of the birds featured in this guide are cavity-nesters and may be enticed to use a birdhouse that you can either build yourself or purchase at a nature or feed store. There is no such thing as a generic nest box – different birds have different needs, and each nest box has to meet the demands of its occupant or it will not be used. The size of the opening and its height above the floor are critical, as is the height of the nest box above the ground. Some nest boxes also serve as winter roost boxes for smaller birds. It may take a season or two to attract wrens and other species to your nest boxes. Once they start nesting on your property, you will enjoy watching the behavior of these nesting birds. Take care that the nest boxes you provide don't simply serve to augment populations of aggressive, non-native species such as European Starlings and House Sparrows.

Hygiene

Feeders, the ground below the feeders, and birdbaths need to be cleaned on a regular basis to avoid the possibility of transmitting avian diseases. The National Audubon Society recommends cleaning your feeders with a solution of one part white vinegar to four parts water. Soap or bleach traces left in feeders may harm hummingbirds, even after a thorough rinsing.

Always wash your hands after taking care of your feeders. Use a shovel, not bare hands, to pick up seeds on the ground or dead birds, and dispose of them in the trash. If there are a number of dead or sick birds at your feeders call your state fish and wildlife people or the local health department, and stop feeding the birds for awhile.

Be sure to inspect nest boxes each fall and give them a good cleaning, but use no insecticides. Discard used nesting materials. Repair any damage so the boxes are ready and waiting for their new occupants to arrive in spring.

Bird Habitats in the Inland Northwest and Northern Rockies

The physical space or environment where a bird or other living creature is normally found is termed its "habitat." Birds as a group occupy a wide diversity of habitats, but individual species often utilize only very specific habitat types. To a large extent, the secret to finding and identifying birds is to study bird habitats and become familiar with the species of birds that are associated with them. The more types of habitats you explore, the greater the variety of birds you will see.

The Inland Northwest and Northern Rockies have the following seven major habitat categories:

CONIFEROUS FORESTS

From majestic ponderosa pine-studded foothills to mountain top stands of whitebark pine and subalpine fir, this habitat offers incredible bird viewing diversity. Our national forests, Glacier and Yellowstone National Parks, and Craters of the Moon National Monument offer opportunities to see Dusky Grouse, Northern Goshawk, Great Gray Owl, Lewis's Woodpecker, Clark's Nutcracker, Varied Thrush, Townsend's Warbler, and White-winged Crossbill.

FARMLAND AND PASTURES

These variable, man-made habitats may not support many nesting species, but often provide food or resting areas for resident and migrating birds. When in farmland habitats watch for Greater White-fronted Goose, Gray Partridge, Ring-necked Pheasant, Northern Harrier, Swainson's Hawk, American Kestrel, Franklin's Gull, American Crow, Horned Lark, Barn Swallow, Savannah Sparrow and Snow Bunting.

LAKES, RESERVOIRS, AND MARSHES

The area's upland habitats, marshes and open water areas are vitally important to nesting and migratory waterfowl. Camas National Wildlife Refuge and Lake Pend Oreille in Idaho, Ninepipe Wildlife

Management Area in Montana, and Malheur National Wildlife Refuge in Oregon offer world class birding for a great variety of waders, waterfowl, and shorebirds.

PARKS AND RESIDENTIAL AREAS

Birds abound in parks, greenbelts, and backyards where habitat has been created or where natural habitats have been preserved and offer the essentials of water, adequate cover, space, and various types of foods. A wide variety of birds are seen in this habitat, among them waterfowl, quail, raptors, and various songbirds.

RIPARIAN AREAS

Riparian areas are unique, essential habitats visited by nearly all of our resident species, as well as many transient, migrating songbirds. These complex and variable seasonal wetlands exist along streams and rivers. They support a mixture of trees, shrubs, and grasses that sustain birds such as Great Blue Heron, Wood Duck, Osprey, Western Screech-Owl, Willow Flycatcher, Eastern Kingbird, American Dipper, Veery, and Yellow-breasted Chat.

SAGEBRUSH DESERT AND GRASSLANDS

Our driest and most open habitats, sagebrush deserts and grasslands consist of interesting mixtures of drought-adapted grasses, forbs, and shrubs. These areas host a variety of birds including Chukar, Greater Sage-Grouse, Ferruginous Hawk, Burrowing Owl, Prairie Falcon, Long-billed Curlew, Common Poorwill, White-throated Swift, Loggerhead Shrike, Sage Thrasher, Brewer's Sparrow, and Western Meadowlark.

SUBALPINE PARKLAND AND ALPINE MEADOWS

Often nearly inaccessible, these high-elevation open forests and meadows can be sampled atop Oregon's Steens Mountain or Logan Pass in Montana's Glacier National Park. Species seen in this habitat might include Olive-sided Flycatcher, American Pipit, Lincoln's and White-crowned Sparrows, Gray-crowned and Black Rosy-Finches.

Birding in the Inland Northwest and Northern Rockies

One of the best ways to see new birds is to join your local National Audubon Society chapter or another nature club on a field trip. Participants often visit new areas, learn how to identify new birds, and meet people who share a common interest. After studying the birds in your yard, visit local parks and greenbelts. A selection of top birding locations in the Inland Northwest and Northern Rockies area is listed below. For maps and directions to these and other fine regional birding sites, consult the bird finding guides and other resources listed on page 14.

Eastern Oregon: Cascade Lakes Highway, Cold Springs and Indian Ford Campgrounds, Hart Mountain National Antelope Refuge, Klamath Basin, Ladd Marsh Wildlife Management Area, Malheur National Wildlife Refuge, McNary Wildlife Nature Area, Steens Mountain, Summer Lake Wildlife Area, Sycan Marsh, and the Wallowa Valley.

Eastern Washington: Coppei Creek, Fields Spring State Park, Kamiak Butte County Park, Lyons Ferry State Park, Potholes Reservoir, Sanpoil River Valley, Soap Lake, Steptoe Butte State Park, Sullivan Lake, Walla Walla River delta, and Yakima River delta.

Idaho: American Falls Reservoir, Boise Greenbelt and parks, Camas National Wildlife Refuge, C.J. Strike Reservoir, Hagerman Wildlife Management Area, Market Lake Wildlife Management Area, Lake Coeur d'Alene, Lake Lowell, Lewiston area, Owyhee County desert and uplands, Sandpoint area, and Ted Trueblood Wildlife Management Area.

Western Montana: Beartooth Highway, Canyon Ferry Reservoir, Ennis Lake, Flathead Lake, Georgetown Lake, Glacier National Park, Lee Metcalf National Wildlife Refuge, National Bison Range, Ninepipe National Wildlife Refuge, Red Rocks National Wildlife Refuge, and Yellowstone National Park.

Helpful Resources

REGIONAL PUBLICATIONS

Burrows, R. and J. Gilligan. *Birds of Oregon*. 2003. Lone Pine Publishing, Auburn, Washington.

Marshall, D. B., G. Hunter and A. Contreras. 2003. *Birds of Oregon: A General Reference*. Oregon State University Press, Corvallis, Oregon.

Opperman, H. 2003. *A Birder's Guide to Washington*. American Birding Association, Colorado Springs, Colorado.

Putnam, C. and G. Kennedy. 2005. *Montana Birds*. Lone Pine Publishing, Auburn, Washington.

Svingen, D. and K. Dumroese. 2005. *The Idaho Bird Guide: What, Where, When*. Backeddy Books, Cambridge, Idaho.

Wahl, T., B. Tweit, and S. Mlodinow. 2005. *Birds of Washington: Status and Distribution*. Oregon State University Press, Corvallis, Oregon.

IDENTIFICATION GUIDES

Kaufman, K. 2000. *Birds of North America*. Houghton Mifflin, New York, New York.

National Geographic Society. 2006. *Field Guide to the Birds of North America, 5th ed.* National Geographic Society, Washington, D.C.

Peterson, R. T. 1990. *A Field Guide to Western Birds, 3rd ed.* Houghton Mifflin, Boston, Massachusetts.

Sibley, D. A. 2003. *The Sibley Field Guide to Birds of Western North America*. Alfred A. Knopf, New York, New York.

JOURNALS

North American Birds (an indispensable quarterly report of bird sightings and related articles and summaries; published by the American Birding Association)

Oregon Birds (the journal of the Oregon Field Ornithologists, published quarterly – an outstanding resource for beginning birders)

Western Birds (the quarterly journal of the Western Field Ornithologists; research papers, bird records committee reports, distribution and identification analyses, with many contributions from amateurs)

WOS Newsletter (bi-monthly publication of the Washington Ornithological Society)

OTHER BIRDING RESOURCES

Cornell Laboratory of Ornithology's BirdSource, including Christmas Bird Counts, Great Backyard Bird Count, Feeder Watch, eBird and other citizen science projects: http://www.birdsource.org.

Idaho Birds (at http://www.idahobirds.net) is a comprehensive on-line resource for birds and birding in Idaho.

NATURE CENTERS, NATURE STORES AND INFORMATION CENTERS

There are a number of great nature centers and stores throughout the Inland Northwest and Northern Rockies. Their staffs are always eager to answer your bird and bird-feeding questions. The yellow pages of the telephone directory or web search engines will locate the closest nature store, such as:

Eastern Oregon: Wild Birds Unlimited store in Bend. Malheur Environmental Field Station Store. The Bobolink in La Grande.

Eastern Washington: McNary National Wildlife Refuge Education Center.

Idaho: MK Nature Center, Boise. Bird House & Habitat, Boise. Wild Birds Unlimited stores in Boise and Coeur d'Alene.

Western Montana: Beartooth Nature Center, Red Lodge. Montana Natural History Center, Missoula. Summit Nature Center, Whitefish. Wild Birds Unlimited stores in Bozeman and Missoula.

Species Accounts

The following pages present accounts and photographs of the most familiar bird species of the Inland Northwest and Northern Rockies Region. Information on each species is presented in a standardized format; see the sample page (opposite) for an explanation. Species are grouped by families, color-coded and thumb-indexed. The Quick Guide to Local Birds (inside the front cover) will help you locate bird families.

Concerning the selection of species in this book, we have tried to include accounts for all commonly observed species that are year-round residents or annual visitors (in winter, migration, the breeding season, or some combination of these).

In addition, we have included some species that are less common or found only in a few localities but which are especially sought-after species in our area. We have chosen to do this in part to convey the tremendous diversity of bird life in our area and to challenge observers to go to the next level and seek out these less numerous species. Not all rare species are included in this guide.

The following terms are used to describe the relative abundance of each species and the likelihood of finding it in a particular season. These definitions were developed by the American Birding Association.

- **Common:** Found in moderate to large numbers, and easily seen in appropriate habitat at the right time of year.
- **Fairly Common:** Found in small to moderate numbers, and usually easy to find in appropriate habitat at the right time of year.
- **Uncommon:** Found in small numbers, and usually—but not always—seen with some effort in appropriate habitat at the right time of year.
- **Rare:** Occurs annually in very small numbers. Not to be expected on any given day, but may be found with extended effort over the course of the appropriate season(s).

Birds shown in the photographs in the Species Accounts are adults unless the captions indicate otherwise

NAME OF THE SPECIES
Its Scientific Name

Description: Length (and wingspan for larger species), followed by a description that includes differences in plumages between sexes and ages. Key field marks—unique markings or structural characteristics visible in the field that help distinguish one species from another—are indicated by boldfaced type.

Similar Species: Identifies similar-appearing species and describes how to differentiate them.

Voice: Describes the main calls and songs of the species. These can be very important for species identification. Note that most species have a much greater vocal repertoire than described here.

Where to Find: Describes the general locations and habitats where this bird may be found in our area, often with suggestions of good places to search for this species. Identifies the times of year that the species is present and its relative abundance (see facing page for definitions of abundance terms).

Behavior: Highlights behavioral characteristics of the species, including feeding behavior, distinctive movements and displays, flight style, and breeding behavior.

Did You Know? Provides other interesting facts about the species.

Date and Location Seen: A place for you to record the date and location of your first sighting of this species.

Immature

Adult

Description: 28", wingspan 53". **Gray-brown goose** with a **pinkish bill** and bright **orange legs**. The **rear underparts are contrastingly white**, and there is a **white band across the base of the tail**; has narrow white tail tip. ADULT: Has **white feathering at the base of the bill, irregular black blotches or speckles across the belly**. JUVENILE: Lacks white on the face and black belly speckles.

Similar Species: Similar-looking domestic geese lack black belly speckles. Canada Goose (p. 23) has a black neck, bill, legs, and broad white chin strap.

Voice: Common flight call is high, yelping *kah-la-luck*.

Where to Find: Fairly common spring (February-April) and fall (October-November) migrant in eastern Oregon and Washington, and southwestern Idaho. Rarely seen elsewhere or at other times of the year. Major migration stops are in Klamath Basin, Summer Lake W.M.A., and Harney Basin in Oregon; McNary N.W.R., Washington; and Fort Boise W.M.A, Idaho.

Behavior: Migrating flocks stage in farm fields along the flyway. Feeds by gleaning grain from fields, grazing grasses, and foraging in shallow water.

Did you Know? These beautiful geese are called "speckle-bellies" by hunters.

Date and Location Seen: _____

_____

Snow Goose Immature

Snow Goose Adult

Ross's Goose Immature

Ross's Goose Adult

Description: 28"/23", wingspan 53"/45". SNOW: **Medium-large white goose with black wingtips. Pink bill** shows black **"grinning patch"** along the sides where the mandibles meet. Juvenile is washed in gray on neck, back, and wings; bill is dull pinkish-gray. Less common "Blue" plumage morph is variably slate-gray on back, breast, and neck. ROSS'S: **Mallard-size** version of Snow Goose, with **smaller, stubbier bill** that **lacks "grinning patch"** and is **blue-gray at base**; juvenile has only limited gray on crown, back, wings. "Blue" plumage morph is very rare.

Similar Species: Larger Swans and white domestic geese do not have black wing tips.

Voice: Call is raucous, fairly high yelping *wowk* or *wow*.

Where to Find: Both species share migration stops along a narrow flyway from their Canadian Arctic nesting sites to their wintering grounds in California. Uncommon to rare away from the flyway. Major stops are at Freezout Lake, Montana; Market Lake W.M.A., Idaho; Klamath Basin, Summer Lake W.M.A. and Harney Basin, Oregon; and Whitcomb Island, Washington. Migrations occur March-April and October-November.

Behavior: Both graze on grasses, grain, and marsh vegetation; they forage in shallow water as well as on land.

Did you Know? Populations of both Snow and Ross's Geese have now become so large that they are heavily impacting their fragile Arctic nesting areas.

Date and Location Seen: _____

_____

Canada Goose
Adult

Cackling Goose

Description: 43"/22", wingspan 60"/43". CANADA: Large brown goose with a pale breast, **black neck, white "chin strap"**, and **flat crown**. Undertail and band across rump are white. Bill and legs are black. CACKLING: Smaller version of Canada, but with darker underparts. Has **small, stubby bill, rounded crown**, and higher, squeakier calls.

Similar Species: Greater White-fronted Goose (p. 19) lacks white "chin strap".

Voice: CANADA: Loud, resonant *ha-ronk*. CACKLING: High-pitched, squeaking *ur-lik*.

Where to Find: CANADA: Common migrants (October to May) and residents of valleys. Winter mainly in low-elevation valleys where food and open water are available. CACKLING: Uncommon to rare winter residents (October to May) that join Canada Goose flocks.

Behavior: Both forage for plants, grains, and invertebrates in wetlands, reservoirs, farmland, and parks. Canada Geese feed and nest in many types of open habitats that provide abundant food resources, water, and sufficient space. Often nests high off the ground on Osprey nest platforms or cliff ledges above water. Aggressive and territorial in breeding season, Canada Geese form large post-breeding flocks that are joined by Cackling Geese in late fall.

Did you Know? At least 11 subspecies of Canada Geese were formerly recognized in North America, but in 2004 the four smallest subspecies were elevated to full species status now known as Cackling Geese.

Date and Location Seen: _____

Tundra Swan

Trumpeter Swan

Description: 52"/60", wingspan 66"/80". **Large white, long-necked** waterfowl with black bills. TUNDRA: Our smallest swan. Crown is rounded, bill profile slightly concave; **forehead feathers form rounded border with bill between eyes**; eyes more distinct from black at bill base; **yellow patch often** (but not always) **shows in front of eye**. Immature is white during spring migration. TRUMPETER: Our largest swan. **Crown and bill profile relatively flat; forehead feathers extend to a point between the eyes**; eyes contained within the black at bill base. Immature retains gray plumage through spring migration.

Similar Species: Smaller Snow Goose (p. 21) has black wing-tips. Introduced Mute Swan (not shown) has distinctive orange bill with black knob at base.

Voice: TUNDRA: Clear, barking *klooo* or *kwooo*. TRUMPETER: Lower-pitched, like trumpet.

Where to Find: TUNDRA: Common migrant (October-November, February-April). Regularly winters at a few locations in southern Idaho and Oregon. TRUMPETER: Rare migrant and winter visitor, usually seen among Tundra flocks. Permanent resident in portions of Montana and eastern Idaho. Breeds at Turnbull N.W.R., Washington and Malheur N.W.R., Oregon.

Behavior: Both typically forage on aquatic plants, seeds and waste grains. Gregarious, often form flocks of both species. Often roost on open water.

Did you Know? Trumpeter Swans were hunted to near extinction by the early 20th century, but now populations are generally increasing.

Date and Location Seen: _____

_____

Male

Female

WOOD DUCK
Aix sponsa

Description: 18.5", wingspan 30". A distinctive duck with **drooping crest**; appears **long tailed** in flight. BREEDING MALE: **Colorful** green, black, and white head pattern; **red bill base and eye ring**; deep reddish breast bordered behind by vertical black and white bars; glossy black upperparts, tan-yellow sides, and iridescent blue wing patch. NON-BREEDING MALE: (Summer, fall) much duller but retains basic pattern. FEMALE: Conspicuous **white patch surrounds eye**, pointed in rear. Gray above, gray spotted with white below.

Similar Species: Female Hooded Merganser (p. 51) lacks white around eye, streaking on body; has white, not green, in speculum. Escaped exotic female Mandarin Ducks lack large white eye patch and have shorter crests.

Voice: Calls include various high whistles, squeaks. Female's call is a penetrating squeal *ooEEK*.

Where to Find: Locally uncommon. Most shift to protected sites in valleys after breeding season. Easily seen in winter at McNary N.W.R., Washington and along Boise River in Boise, Idaho.

Behavior: Often perches in trees over water, usually in secluded forested wetlands. Feeds on invertebrates, seeds, and fruits in shallow water; does not dive. Nests in natural tree cavities or nest boxes.

Did you Know? Although Wood Ducks prefer scarce natural tree cavities for nesting, they will readily use nest boxes.

Date and Location Seen: _____

Eurasian Wigeon
Male

American Wigeon
Male

American Wigeon
Female

Description: 18", wingspan 32". Medium-size dabbling ducks with short, black-tipped, bluish-gray bills, white forewing patches, and relatively long, pointed tails. Males of both species have white flank patches and **black undertails**. AMERICAN: Male has **grayish head** with **bright green patch behind eye** and **white or buffy forehead**; has **pinkish-brown back and flanks**. Female has grayish-brown head, brown breast and flanks, white belly. EURASIAN: Male has **dark rufous head with yellowish forehead, gray back and flanks**. Female has cinnamon-brown head.

Similar Species: Female Cinnamon Teal (p. 33) has darker, longer bill. Gadwall (p. 31) has white wing patch, longer yellowish bill.

Voice: AMERICAN: Whistle is *wi-WE-whew*. EURASIAN: Single descending whistle is *wEEEEEEr*.

Where to Find: AMERICAN: Uncommon breeder, common migrant, and locally abundant winter resident from September to May. Major wintering areas include Columbia Basin, Washington and Klamath Basin, Oregon. EURASIAN: Rare winter resident that accompanies American Wigeon flocks. Both species regularly winter in Boise, Idaho.

Behavior: Both eat mostly plant material, often grazing lawns or fields. Regularly feed on grass In residential parks and golf courses. Also forage in ponds and marshes by skimming surface, rarely dipping. Form large post-breeding season flocks.

Did you Know? American Wigeon are also known as "Baldpates".

Date and Location Seen: ───────────────

───────────────────────────────

Mallard Male

Mallard Female

Gadwall Male

Gadwall Female

Description: 23"/20", wingspan 35"/33". MALLARD: Large, heavy-bodied, with blue speculum bordered in front and back by white; white underwings, orange legs. Male has **green head, white neck ring, reddish breast**, pale gray body, curled black feathers at base of tail; bill yellow. Female is mottled brown, with dark line through eye, orange and dusky bill. GADWALL: Medium-size, plain duck with squarish head, orange legs, white belly, **square white patch on speculum of wing**. Male is **variegated gray** with paler gray head, **black rear end**; dark gray bill. Female is mottled brown and white; **orange sides to bill**; white wing patch visible at rest.

Similar Species: Female Northern Shoveler (p. 35) has blue forewing and longer, wider bill. Female American Wigeon (p. 29) has rich, orangish-brown, unmottled breast and gray bill.

Voice: MALLARD: Female gives familiar *quack*. GADWALL: Female has a higher-pitched, more nasal *quack*.

Where to Find: Both species are common widespread breeders, migrants, and winter residents. The main wintering areas are Columbia and Klamath Basins, and Snake River Valley in Idaho.

Behavior: Both species forage for vegetation in shallow water by "tipping up"; also graze on land. MALLARD: Nests near water, increasingly in residential areas. GADWALL: Favors shallow marshes and ponds containing aquatic plants.

Did you Know? Nearly all domestic ducks were derived from Mallards.

Date and Location Seen: _____

_____

Blue-winged Teal
Female

Blue-winged Teal
Male

Cinnamon Teal
Male

Cinnamon Teal
Female

Description: 16", wingspan 23". Small dabbling ducks with long, wide dark bill, **pale blue forewing patch** and green speculum (visible in flight), and orange-yellow legs. BLUE-WINGED: Male has spotted brown body with a **slate-gray head and bold white face crescent and flank patch**, and black undertail. Female is mottled brown with diffuse, pale facial area behind bill. CINNAMON: Male is **deep cinnamon-red nearly throughout**; has red eyes, black undertail. Female is mottled brown with a plain brown head.

Similar Species: Smaller female Green-winged Teal (p. 39) lacks blue forewing. Northern Shoveler (p. 35) is similar, but has oversized, spatulate bill.

Voice: Females *quack*, males give low chatter.

Where to Find: CINNAMON: Common migrants and summer breeders (April to mid-October). More common in the south. BLUE-WINGED: Fairly common migrants and summer breeders; more abundant in the northern portion of our region. Both are rare in winter.

Behavior: Both species forage in small, shallow wetlands with dense aquatic plants, and nest in low, grassy vegetation near water.

Did you Know? Blue-winged and Cinnamon Teal are closely related and occasionally interbreed.

Date and Location Seen: _____

_____

Male

Male

Female

Description: 19", wingspan 30". Medium-size dabbler with **large, spatulate bill**. Large bill gives front-heavy appearance in flight. MALE: Has **green head** with yellow eyes, **white breast**, and **cinnamon sides**. In flight shows light blue-gray forewing with broad white rear border. FEMALE: Mottled brown with broad buffy-white edges to side and flank feathers; gray forewing with narrow white rear border. Female's large, spoon-shaped bill has distinctive orange sides.

Similar Species: Many other female ducks look similar, but none have large, expanded bill.

Voice: Females *quack*, males give soft *thup-tup*.

Where to Find: Common migrant (April-May, August-October), fairly common summer resident, and locally common winter resident.

Behavior: Flocks feed in shallow water by tipping up or sifting through water and mud with outsized bills used in sweeping motions. Groups often swim in tight, circling masses with their heads underwater, capturing food stirred up from below. Flocks fly in bunches or loose lines.

Did you Know? Northern Shovelers have fringes along the sides of the bill that help them filter food items from water and mud.

Date and Location Seen: _____

Male

Female

Description: 21", wingspan 33". Slender, **long-necked dabbling duck** with a **gray bill** and long, pointed tail. MALE: **Brown head**, white breast, **white stripes extending up the sides of the neck**. Gray body with elongated black and white feathers on sides of back; black undertail, **long pointed central tail feathers**. Green speculum, bordered in front by buff, behind by white. FEMALE: Plain pale brown head and neck, mottled gray-brown body; **central tail feathers pointed**. In flight shows white trailing edge to inner wing; bill is plain gray.

Similar Species: Other dabbling ducks have shorter, stockier necks and lack the pointed tail. Female Redhead (p. 41) is stockier, more solidly gray-brown on the body, and has pale gray flight feathers.

Voice: Female gives hoarse *quacks*. Male gives a thin, wheezy whistle and a musical *droop* call, often doubled.

Where to Find: Uncommon summer resident and migrant (March-April, September-November), uncommon in winter. Thousands gather on the Walla Walla River delta, Washington in late February.

Behavior: Feeds by tipping up, with long tail pointed skyward and head and neck underwater. Flies in lines or "V"s, appearing slim and long-necked.

Did you Know? Northern Pintails are favorites among birders for their graceful elegance and beauty.

Date and Location Seen: _____

___

Male

Female

Description: 14", wingspan 23". Smallest dabbling duck. All show bright **green speculum** with buffy-white border in front. Bill is small and dark. MALE: **Bright green ear patch** borders **chestnut crown and face**; body is gray with **white vertical stripe behind breast**; undertail is pale yellow and black. FEMALE: Mottled brown; dark line through eye bordered indistinctly by buffy-brown lines; buffy patch is on sides of undertail.

Similar Species: Female Cinnamon (p. 33) and Blue-winged Teal (p. 33) have larger bills and blue-gray forewing patches, lack buff or whitish area below tail.

Voice: Male's call is high *dreep*. Female's call is short, rough *quack*.

Where to Find: Common migrant (March-May, August-October), uncommon summer resident and winter resident throughout. Breeds mainly in river valleys in the northern portion of our region. Thousands gather at the Walla Walla River delta, Washington in spring.

Behavior: Forages by dabbling at surface of shallow water, also feeds shorebird-style on mudflats. Springs vertically from the water when disturbed. Mostly migratory, though many remain farther north during the winter than other species of teal.

Did you Know? Male Eurasian Green-winged Teal (Common Teal) have a white horizontal stripe above the wing instead of the vertical breast stripe. They sometimes appear in winter flocks with American Green-winged Teal.

Date and Location Seen: _____

_____

39

Redhead Male

Canvasback Male

Redhead Female

Canvasback Female

Description: 21″/19″, wingspan 29″. CANVASBACK: Male has **nearly whitish body, deep chestnut head**, red eyes, **long, sloping forehead and long, black bill**. Female is pale gray with light brown head and chest, pale gray wings. RED-HEAD: Male is **medium gray** with **bright rufous-red head**, rounded forehead, and shorter **blue-gray bill with black tip** preceded by a white line. Female is plain gray-brown; **pale gray flight feathers contrast with darker forewing**.

Similar Species: Female Greater and Lesser Scaup (p. 45), Ring-necked Duck (p. 43) similar to female Redhead, but have distinct white patches at the base of their bills.

Voice: Both species generally quiet.

Where to Find: CANVASBACK: Fairly common but local migrant and wintering species (September-April), most common along Columbia and Snake Rivers. Uncommon to rare summer resident, but common in Oregon's Klamath Basin. REDHEAD: Common migrant and summer resident (March-October), regular in southeastern Idaho. Uncommon to rare in winter, except fairly common in southeastern Washington and parts of Idaho.

Behavior: Both species dive underwater in marshes, ponds, and lakes for aquatic plants and invertebrates. They form large, mixed flocks with other wintering diving ducks.

Did you Know? Female Redheads sometimes lay their eggs in the nests of other Redheads, or in the nests of other duck species.

Date and Location Seen: _____

41

Male

Female

Description: 17", wingspan 25". Has gray bill with **white rings at base and near tip**, bill tip is black; **head is peaked at rear of crown**. In flight, gray flight feathers contrast with darker forewing. MALE: Black with **white crescent behind black breast**, has pale gray sides, head glossed purple, chestnut neck ring difficult to see. FEMALE: Slaty above, brown below; has white eye-ring, and diffuse, white feathering at base of bill that contrasts with gray face.

Similar Species: Differs from scaup (p. 45) in having white rings on bill, much more peaked crown, and lacks white wing stripes. Male scaup have gray (not black) back, whitish (not gray) sides; female scaup have distinct white patch at bill base and lack an eye-ring.

Voice: Generally silent.

Where to Find: Common migrant and winter resident (October-April), uncommon breeder and summer resident.

Behavior: Favors shallower water and more heavily vegetated sites where it forages for aquatic plants and invertebrates. Sometimes flocks with scaup and other diving ducks. Usually forms small flocks.

Did you Know? Ring-necked Duck males have bright yellow eyes, whereas the eyes of females are browner.

Date and Location Seen: _____

_____

Greater Scaup Female

Greater Scaup Male

Lesser Scaup Female

Lesser Scaup Male

Description: 18"/17", wingspan 28"/26". Short-necked diving ducks with bluish-gray bills and **white wing stripes** visible in flight. MALES: **Blackish on both ends, whitish in middle**, head darkly iridescent. FEMALES: Brownish with **white facial patch at bill base**. GREATER: **Head** is **round**, neck thicker, bill wider, male's head glosses greenish. LESSER: **Peaked crown**, neck thinner, bill smaller, **wing stripe extends only halfway to wingtip**, male's head glosses purple.

Similar Species: Ring-necked Duck (p. 43) head is more peaked, has ring near bill tip; male has black back, vertical white mark on side.

Voice: Grating sounds, deep whistles.

Where to Find: GREATER: Uncommon to rare migrant (April-May, September-November), winter resident, except common along Columbia River. LESSER: Common migrant and winter resident (September-May). Most common in winter along the Columbia and Snake Rivers. Uncommon local summer resident, most expected in Klamath Basin, Oregon.

Behavior: Both dive for mollusks, other aquatic animals, plants. Highly gregarious, gathering in tight flocks, often including both scaup species, other ducks. LESSER: Nests in shallow wetlands, with nest constructed on nearby dry uplands. In winter, most often seen on larger open rivers and lakes, including sewage ponds.

Did you Know? Hunters refer to both scaup as "bluebills".

Date and Location Seen: _____

_____

Male

Female

Description: 13", wingspan 21". Our **smallest duck**, with a small, gray bill. MALE: White below and mostly black above. Has a large **white area on the back of its head** and a large white wing patch. FEMALE: Dark gray throughout with an **oval white cheek patch** and a small white speculum.

Similar Species: Larger Common Goldeneye (p. 49) male has white patch at base of bill; female is gray-bodied and lacks white cheek patch.

Voice: Generally silent.

Where to Find: Common migrant and winter resident (November-May). Major migration stops are in southeast Idaho and the Klamath Basin, Oregon. Uncommon and local in summer in Cascade and Rocky Mountains lakes.

Behavior: Dives for aquatic invertebrates and small fish in small, loose flocks. Nests in tree cavities or duck nesting boxes at high-elevation forested lakes. Widespread in winter at lowland lakes and sewage ponds.

Did you Know? Buffleheads rarely leave the water to walk on the ground.

Date and Location Seen: _____

_____

Common Goldeneye Male

Common Goldeneye Female

Barrow's Goldeneye Male

Barrow's Goldeneye Female

Description: 18", wingspan 27". Chunky, medium-size diving ducks with **white patches at the base of the wings** and yellow eyes. Males are mostly white with black and white upperparts; have dark, iridescent, puffy heads with white face patches. Females are grayish with brown heads. COMMON: **Green head** is **peaked in middle of crown**; has **round white face patch**; has less black on back. BARROW'S: **Purplish head** is **peaked at forehead**; has **crescent-shaped white face patch**. Bill is smaller; has rows of white spots on black back.

Similar Species: Smaller male Bufflehead (p. 47) has large white patch on back of its head.

Voice: Generally silent. Females of both species give low, grating *arr arr* calls.

Where to Find: COMMON: Common migrant and winter resident (October-May). Winters on the Columbia and Snake Rivers and rivers in western Montana. Rare in summer with occasional nesting. BARROW'S: Uncommon to fairly common migrant and winter resident (October-April), uncommon and local breeder. Wintering concentrations occur near Lewiston, Idaho and on large rivers in western Montana.

Behavior: Both mainly consume aquatic invertebrates. Usually nest in tree cavities along forest-edged lakes, ponds, and streams. Both commonly lay eggs in nests of other goldeneyes, sometimes in nests of other cavity-nesting ducks species.

Did you Know? Goldeneye wings produce a loud whistling sound in flight.

Date and Location Seen: ⎯⎯⎯⎯⎯⎯⎯⎯⎯⎯⎯⎯

⎯⎯⎯⎯⎯⎯⎯⎯⎯⎯⎯⎯⎯⎯⎯⎯⎯⎯⎯⎯⎯⎯⎯⎯⎯⎯

Male

Female

Description: 18". Small, thin-billed, long-tailed diving duck. MALE: **Puffy white crest is outlined in black**; when folded back, white of crest is reduced to a long, thick stripe. Black above, tawny on sides, with **two vertical black bars on sides of white breast**. FEMALE: Dusky above, gray-brown on breast and sides; belly is white; **puffy light tawny-brown crest**; bill has much yellow on sides. Immature male like female but with black bill and a hint of adult's head pattern.

Similar Species: Bufflehead (p. 47) has bright white sides with a stubby gray bill. Other mergansers are much larger with red bills.

Voice: Generally silent, males emit frog-like croaks during courtship.

Where to Find: Fairly common and widespread migrant, uncommon to rare summer resident. Uncommon and local winter resident (October-March) in open water areas.

Behavior: Dives for small fish and aquatic invertebrates. Nests in tree cavities and nest boxes along woodland streams, swamps, and ponds. Secretive during the nesting season; they move to open water areas in winter where they sometimes form small flocks.

Did you Know? They sometimes lay their eggs in the nest cavities of other Hooded Mergansers or even those of other cavity-nesting ducks.

Date and Location Seen: _____

Common Merganser
Male

Common Merganser
Female

Red-Breasted Merganser
Male

Red-Breasted Merganser
Female

Description: 25"/23", wingspan 34"/30". Diving ducks with long, slender bills that have saw-like edges. COMMON: **Bill deep-based** and **bright red**. Adult male has **green head** with short, smooth crest; **body mostly white** with black down center of back. Female and young male have **deep rusty head and neck sharply separated from white chin and chest**; gray breast and flanks. RED-BREASTED: **Bill reddish-orange**. Adult male has **dark green head with shaggy, thin crest**, white neck ring, mottled reddish-brown breast bordered behind by black and white patch; mostly blackish above, gray and white below with much white in the wing. Female and young male show **tawny brown head with thin, shaggy crest**, gray body.

Similar Species: Only likely to be confused with each other.

Voice: Both species are usually silent, but male Common makes low croaking calls.

Where to Find: COMMON: Fairly common migrant and winter resident (October-May), mainly in Idaho and Montana. Uncommon summer resident, mostly on large rivers and reservoirs. RED-BREASTED: Uncommon to rare migrant and winter resident (September-May), mainly on large ice-free rivers and reservoirs.

Behavior: Both species dive for fish, which they catch and hold with their "saw-toothed" bills. Sometimes flocks move together, herding fish.

Did you Know? Merganser "teeth" are simply projections on the horny covering of the bill, and not actually teeth.

Date and Location Seen: ───────────────────

───────────────────────────────────────

Breeding Male

Female

Description: 15". Small duck with a long, **stiff tail, often pointed upward**. MALE: Blackish crown, **large white cheek patch**. Mainly gray-brown (darker above), except the **body is entirely deep chestnut-colored** and **bill is sky blue** when breeding. FEMALE: Resembles non-breeding male, but with **dark line across whitish cheek**.

Similar Species: Female Bufflehead (p. 47) is grayer with smaller white cheek patch and shorter tail.

Voice: Male displays with an accelerating series of low, popping notes ending in a low croak: *fup fup fup fup fuf-fuf-fuf-frrrrrp.*

Where to Find: Common summer resident and migrant (September-October, March-April) with concentrations in Klamath Basin, Oregon and southeastern Idaho. Fairly common, but local in winter where large bodies of water remain open.

Behavior: Dives for aquatic plants, as well as small fish and invertebrates. More likely to dive than fly when approached. Displaying males point tails straight upward and bob their heads in time with vocalizations.

Did you Know? The Ruddy Duck is a member of the "stiff-tail" ducks. Unlike other ducks that molt into their brightest plumage during winter, the stiff-tails are brightest in summer and dullest in winter.

Date and Location Seen: _____

Chukar

Gray Partridge

Description: 14"/12.5", wingspan 20"/19". Medium-size, chunky introduced game birds of dry, open areas. CHUKAR: Male and female alike. Pale gray overall, with **cream-colored face and throat outlined in black**; short, red bill and legs. **Bold dark barring on buffy flanks**, buffy belly, pale cinnamon undertail, short rufous tail. GRAY: **Grayish-brown** overall, with **rufous face** (female's is buff), **bold rufous bars and pale streaks on flanks**, gray bill. Male has **chestnut belly patch**, absent on female.

Similar Species: Mountain Quail (p. 69) has rusty flanks barred with white, chestnut throat and dark bill.

Voice: CHUKAR: Call is *kucka-kucka-kucka* series. GRAY: Call is hoarse *keeeah*.

Where to Find: CHUKAR: Fairly common resident of arid, rocky foothills and canyons that support a mixture of shrubs, grasses, and forbs. GRAY: Uncommon, secretive resident of farmlands and adjacent grassy uplands. Both may be seen south of Boise, Idaho; at Sun Lakes S.P., Washington; and Succor Creek, Oregon.

Behavior: Both species gregarious; post-breeding flocks forage within their respective habitats. CHUKAR: Diet is mainly leaves and insects in summer, grass and forb seeds in winter. GRAY: Eats seeds, waste grain, leaves, and insects.

Did you Know? Both natives of Eurasia, the first Chukars were introduced to North America in 1893, and the release of Gray Partridges first began in the early 1900s.

Date and Location Seen: _____

_____

Male

Female

Description: 21-35", wingspan 31". Medium-size **game bird** with a **long, pointed tail**. Male is strikingly mottled brown, with dark-spotted, orange flanks, pale-spotted rust back, gray rump, **broad, white neck-ring, iridescent green head**, and **red facial skin**. Female is mottled brown with a long tail.

Similar Species: Larger Greater Sage-Grouse (p. 63) has black belly. Smaller Sharp-tailed Grouse (p. 63) has a shorter tail, prominent white wing spots, and white tail base.

Voice: Males give loud, harsh cackle *uurk-iik*, issued in long, rapid series when flushed.

Where to Find: Fairly common introduced resident of low-elevation valleys. Typically found in cropland, marshes, and pastures interspersed with or adjacent to dense cover with water. Common in the Columbia Basin and along the Snake River.

Behavior: Forages for insects, seeds, agricultural grains, and other foods. Generally runs from intruders into protective cover, but a strong flier when flushed. Nests on the ground in tall vegetation. Often forms large post-breeding flocks.

Did you Know? The first successful introduction of Ring-necked Pheasants in the United States was in Oregon's Willamette Valley in 1882.

Date and Location Seen: _____

_____

Description: 18". Slender forest grouse. **Mottled** and spotted **brownish-gray** overall, with **bold, dark vertical bars on flanks**. Finely-barred **tail has wide, dark band near tip**, is relatively long and somewhat rounded. **Head is crested**, though crest is sometimes flattened. Males have large, **dark neck ruffs** exposed when displaying during breeding season, inconspicuous at other times.

Similar Species: Larger Dusky Grouse (p. 65) has tail with dark gray band at the tip. Smaller Spruce Grouse (p. 65) has an all-dark tail.

Voice: Nasal squeals, clucks.

Where to Find: Fairly common resident of moist deciduous and mixed forests with dense understories, especially riparian areas.

Behavior: Mostly feeds on buds and other plant materials, lesser amounts of insects and other invertebrates. "Drumming" male produces low-pitched, accelerating wingbeat sounds during spring breeding display, usually from atop a log. Male also erects crest and neck ruff, fan tail when displaying. Nests on the ground, usually at the base of a tree or stump. Family groups often seen feeding along forest roadways. Female aggressively defends brood with an elaborate distraction display. Solitary in winter.

Did you Know? Ruffed Grouse are polygamous; male may breed with several females that are attracted to his drumming. Then after copulation, the females build their nests and raise their young without any assistance from the male.

Date and Location Seen: _____

_____

Greater Sage-Grouse
Male Displaying

Greater Sage-Grouse
Female

Sharp-tailed Grouse

Description: 22"-28"/17", wingspan 33"-38"/25". SAGE: **Large**, with **long, pointed tail**. Mottled **brownish-gray** with white patterning; **black belly**. Breeding male has yellow eyebrows, black throat, white breast; shows long head plumes and expanding large orange air sacs on chest. Female is similar with pale throat and grayish-brown breast. White underwings visible in flight. SHARP-TAIL: **Medium-size. Upperparts** and breast **mottled brown with white spots; underparts pale with dark chevrons on flanks; head is slightly crested; short, pointed tail** has white base. Displaying male shows yellowish eyebrows and pinkish-purple air sacs on sides of neck.

Similar Species: Both differentiated from other grouse by their pointed tails.

Voice: Both usually quiet. SAGE: Displaying males produce eerie *oo-WIdoo-WIdoo-wup* popping hoots on leks. SHARP-TAIL: Displaying males produce high-pitched hoots; both sexes give clucking calls.

Where to Find: Residents of open upland areas. SAGE: Uncommon to rare in sagebrush areas. SHARP-TAIL: Rare in grassland and shrub habitats, especially mountain shrub and sagebrush habitats. SAGE: Found in Beaverhead County, Montana and Hart Mountain N.W.R., Oregon. Both seen in Washington County, Idaho and Douglas County, Washington.

Behavior: Both forage mainly for plant materials and consume insects. Males gather at leks each spring (March-May) to perform elaborate courtship displays.

Did you Know? Both are declining across their geographic range.

Date and Location Seen: _____

Dusky Grouse
Male

Dusky Grouse
Male Displaying

Spruce Grouse
Male

Spruce Grouse
Female

DUSKY GROUSE/SPRUCE GROUSE
Dendragapus obscurus / Falcipennis canadensis

Description: 20"/16", wingspan 26"/22". DUSKY: Large, long-necked, and long-tailed. Male is **sooty-brown above and bluish-gray below** with pale spotting on flanks and belly; **yellow combs above eyes; blackish tail has dark gray band at tip**. Smaller female mottled gray-brown with pale spots on flanks and belly. SPRUCE: Medium-size, stocky, short-necked, and short-tailed. Male dark-barred brown above, **black below with prominent white spots on flanks and belly**. Eyes have **red combs above and white arcs below. Tail black**. Female rufous-brown, with dark barring on brown and white underparts, dark tail.

Similar Species: Female Spruce Grouse lacks tail bands and is darker than Ruffed Grouse (p. 61).

Voice: Both species cluck and produce low hoots.

Where to Find: DUSKY: Uncommon resident of coniferous forests and nearby grasslands, shrub habitats. Regular on Boise Ridge, Idaho and National Bison Range, Montana. SPRUCE: Rare and secretive resident of coniferous forests. Good places include upper McCully Creek near Joseph, Oregon; Sawtooth National Recreation Area, Idaho; Glacier National Park, Montana.

Behavior: Both forage on ground for plant material and insects. SPRUCE: Also forages in trees. Both males have elaborate breeding displays and calls. DUSKY: After breeding, migrates upslope to dense conifer stands where they winter.

Did you Know? Spruce Grouse seem unafraid of humans and sometimes feed or display while people stand over them.

Date and Location Seen: _____

Male

Female

WILD TURKEY
Meleagris gallopavo

Description: 36-47", wingspan 50-64". **Large**, familiar forest bird. MALE: **Overall dark**, wings barred black and white; **head and neck skin bluish-gray with numerous pink wattles**; long, black "beard" projects from breast; rump and tail feathers tipped with buff or whitish; legs are pink, stout; bill short and down-curved. FEMALE and IMMATURE: Smaller; dark plumage tipped buff or whitish; has short "beard" or none; head has short feathers and small, dull wattles.

Similar Species: Domestic turkey is usually larger, plumper, often all-white.

Voice: Displaying male gives familiar descending *gobble*, females give *tuk* and series of *yike* calls;

Where to Find: Introduced locally common resident, mostly in lower elevation foothills and mountains. Usually found in open coniferous, deciduous, or mixed shrub/grassland habitats with water nearby.

Behavior: Forages on ground (often by scratching) for seeds, nuts, fruit, insects. Rarely flies, except to roost in trees at night. In breeding display, male puffs out feathers, spreads tail, swells facial wattles, droops wings, and gobbles. Nomadic and gregarious after breeding season, they often gather in large flocks in fall and move to lower elevation areas.

Did you Know? Wild Turkey, native to the eastern half of the U.S., was introduced as a gamebird to our region. Populations are still expanding in most areas.

Date and Location Seen: ─────────────

Mountain Quail
Male

California Quail
Male

California Quail
Female

Description: 10"/11". CALIFORNIA: Plump gray gamebird with short, rounded wings, gray tail, small black bill, and **curved black topknot. Belly is scaled with white**, brown flanks with white streaks. Male has **black throat outlined in white**; dark brown crown; conspicuous flared, forward-curved topknot; dark chestnut belly patch. Female has gray-brown head with little patterning; topknot is small, nearly straight. MOUNTAIN: Male and female alike. Large grayish-brown quail with **long, straight plume**, chestnut throat, rufous undertail, and **bold chestnut and white bars** on flanks.

Similar Species: Gambel's Quail (introduced near Salmon, Idaho) similar to California Quail, but with unmarked cream-colored belly.

Voice: CALIFORNIA: Call is *spwik wik wiw*; song a loud *chi CA go*. MOUNTAIN: Call is *kow kow kow* series; song is loud *QUEark*.

Where to Find: CALIFORNIA: Native to the Klamath Basin, Oregon; introduced elsewhere. Common resident of dense shrubby habitats in low-elevation valleys. MOUNTAIN: Uncommon resident of shrub and forest habitats on the east slopes of Cascades in Oregon and southern Washington. Rare and local in Blue Mountains of Oregon, and western Idaho. Populations declining in all areas.

Behavior: Both species forage for seeds, plants, and insects. Form flocks in non-breeding season. Aggressively defend territories and young.

Did you Know? Quail readily use backyard birdfeeders.

Date and Location Seen: _____

_____

69

Pacific Loon
Non-breeding

Common Loon
Juvenile

Common Loon
Breeding

Description: 32"/25", wingspan 46"/36". COMMON: Our **largest loon**, with a **heavy bill**. NON-BREEDING: Gray-brown above, white below. **White partial collar on neck** with broad, dark collar extending forward; white arcs around eyes. BREEDING: Green-glossed **black head and bill**; collar of white vertical bars on neck, black collar below; **checkered black and white back**. PACIFIC: Medium-size loon with straight bill. NON-BREEDING: Dark brown upperparts, crown and **neck sides contrast sharply with white throat** and underparts. Juveniles barred with gray above and paler gray hindneck. Most show thin, dusky "chinstrap". BREEDING: **Hindneck pale gray, black throat**. Checkered **white patches on back**.

Similar Species: Smaller, paler Red-throated Loon (rare) has thin, upturned bill. Larger Yellow-billed Loon (rare) has paler bill.

Voice: COMMON: Distinctive, low yodels and cries. PACIFIC: Generally silent.

Where to Find: COMMON: Fairly common migrant (September-October, April-May), uncommon in winter. Uncommon to rare in summer with occasional nesting. PACIFIC: Rare fall migrant (October-November), mainly on larger rivers and lakes.

Behavior: Both make long dives for fish. Require secluded lakes with good supply of small fish for breeding. Build mound nests on shorelines or islands, aggressively defend territory. Non-breeding loons loosely congregate in good feeding areas.

Did you Know? Loons are expert swimmers and divers, but walk very awkwardly on land, and cannot take flight from land at all.

Date and Location Seen: _____

_____

Breeding

Non-breeding

Description: 13″. Small diving bird with a **short, thick, chicken-like bill**. Plain tawny brown throughout. BREEDING: Has black throat patch, **whitish bill with black ring near tip**. NON-BREEDING ADULT and IMMATURE: Bill is plain pale brownish. Juveniles and downy young have black and white-striped faces.

Similar Species: Eared Grebe (p. 77) has longer, slimmer neck, thin bill, and more contrasting gray and white plumage. Horned Grebe (p. 75) has flat crown, golden head plumes in summer and white cheeks in winter. American Coot (p. 121) is slaty-gray with a black head and white bill.

Voice: Vocal in summer. Male's song is loud *kuh kuh kuh kow kow kow kow-ah kow-ah*, etc. during breeding season. Interacting birds give chatter *huzza-huzza-huzza*.

Where to Find: Fairly common migrant (March-April, September-October) and summer resident. Uncommon to fairly common winter resident, mostly along the Columbia and Snake Rivers.

Behavior: Dives for fish and aquatic invertebrates. Forages and nests on water bodies with cattails and other aquatic vegetation. Nest is a well-concealed floating platform attached to emergent vegetation. Seen in pairs or family groups, seldom in flocks. Rarely seen in flight.

Did you Know? When disturbed, Pied-billed Grebes slowly sink their bodies and then move quickly away from the source of danger under water, or with just their heads above water like submarine periscopes.

Date and Location Seen: _____

**Horned Grebe
Breeding**

**Horned Grebe
Non-breeding**

**Red-necked Grebe
Breeding**

**Red-necked Grebe
Non-breeding**

Description: 14"/18", wingspan 18"/24". HORNED: Small, compact water bird with **relatively flat crown**. Has **short, thick neck**, red eyes, **straight bill** with light tip, white underparts. BREEDING: **Black head with prominent yellow eye patch, rufous neck** and flanks. NON-BREEDING: Dark gray crown, hindneck and back; **white cheeks, throat and foreneck**. RED-NECKED: **Large** grayish-brown grebe. Wedge-shaped head with dark eyes, long and stout yellowish bill, thick neck, white underparts. BREEDING: **Black crown, whitish cheeks, rufous neck**. NON-BREEDING: Dark crown and back, dingy pale gray and white cheeks and neck.

Similar Species: Eared Grebe (p. 77) rides higher in water than Horned, has rounded crown, dusky neck, grayish cheek patch. Western Grebe (p. 79) is larger than Red-necked; has long, white neck.

Voice: HORNED: Call is *way-err*; song is trilling and squeaky. RED-NECKED: Call is sharp *krik*; song is loud and braying.

Where to Find: Both fairly common migrants (April-May, October-November), locally uncommon to rare in winter. HORNED: Uncommon to rare summer resident. RED-NECKED: Uncommon and local summer resident, mainly in the northern portion of our region.

Behavior: Both dive under water for small fish and a variety of aquatic invertebrates. Nest on open marshes, ponds, or lakes edged with aquatic vegetation. Build floating nests on aquatic vegetation.

Did you Know? Both species perform spectacular, elaborate breeding displays.

Date and Location Seen: ─────────────────────

75

Breeding

Non-Breeding

Description: 13". Small, **slim-necked** grebe with a **thin, slightly up-turned bill** and bright red eyes. Feathering at the rear usually fluffed out when the bird is resting on the water. NON-BREEDING: Gray above and whitish with gray mottling below. **Peaked crown** is dark down to the cheek; the neck is variably washed with gray. BREEDING: Head and neck are black with yellow plumes on the sides of the head. Breast and flanks are chestnut.

Similar Species: Horned Grebe (p. 75) has a flat, black crown, shorter neck with a clean, white foreneck, pale spot in front of the eye, and pale-tipped bill.

Voice: Song is high repeated whistle *ooEEK*.

Where to Find: Locally common summer resident. Common migrant (April-May, August-October) with major concentrations at Malheur N.W.R. and Lake Abert, Oregon and Soap Lake, Washington. Rare in winter.

Behavior: Dives for small fish and aquatic invertebrates. Often found in large flocks, sometimes tightly concentrated. Nests in colonies on shallow vegetated ponds and lake margins. Like most of our grebes, they are rarely seen in flight.

Did you Know? Because Eared Grebes build their nests close to or on the water, the nests are highly vulnerable to strong winds.

Date and Location Seen: _____

_____

Clark's Grebe
Non-breeding

Western Grebe

Description: 25". Largest grebes, with long slender necks and bright red eyes. **Gray above, white foreneck and underparts**, with **black crown**. WESTERN: Has **dull yellow to olive bill; black crown extends over eyes** (patch surrounding eye fades to gray in winter). CLARK'S: Has **bright orange-yellow bill; eye surrounded by white** (grayish connects eye and crown in winter), dark on hindneck is more restricted. Has more extensive white on wings, **paler flanks**.

Similar Species: Smaller Horned Grebe (p. 75) has shorter neck.

Voice: WESTERN: Loud, grating *kree-kreeek*. CLARK'S: Single drawn-out *kreeeek*.

Where to Find: Both species are usually found together. WESTERN: Common summer resident (April-October), uncommon to rare and local in Idaho in winter. CLARK'S: Uncommon to common summer resident (April-October), rare and local in Idaho in winter. Large numbers seen at Upper Klamath Lake and Goose Lake, Oregon; Lake Lowell and Minidoka N.W.R., Idaho; and Potholes Reservoir, Washington.

Behavior: Both dive for fish in marshes, lakes and reservoirs. Displaying birds rush along water surface with gracefully curved necks. Floating nests are anchored to vegetation in marshy pond borders. As in all grebes, downy chicks may ride on backs of parents.

Did you Know? These two species were formerly considered different plumage morphs of a single species.

Date and Location Seen: _____

Description: 50", wingspan 108". **Enormous white waterbird** with **long yellowish-orange bill and expandable throat pouch**. Wings long with **black flight feathers**. Legs orange, feet webbed; has short white tail. Breeding adults have small horn on upper bill. IMMATURE: Like adults, except grayish on head and back.

Similar Species: Much smaller Snow Goose (p. 21) has small, dark bill. Swans have all-white wings and dark bills.

Voice: Generally silent.

Where to Find: Common migrant (April-May, September-October) and locally common summer resident with a tendency to wander. Breeding colonies exist at Minidoka N.W.R., Idaho; Canyon Ferry Reservoir, Montana; and Walla Walla River delta, Washington. Large numbers concentrate at Malheur N.W.R., Oregon in late summer and fall. Some winter at low-elevation rivers and reservoirs.

Behavior: Highly gregarious. Forages for fish in shallow marshes, rivers, reservoirs. Adult often flies long distances daily between nesting grounds and feeding areas. Eats between 20-40% of its weight in fish each day. Requires an undisturbed island and reliable source of abundant fish for nesting. Shy and sensitive at nest sites, prone to abandon nest if disturbed. Flocks often seen flying in formation high overhead.

Did you Know? American White Pelicans often feed cooperatively. Flocks encircle fish or drive them into the shallows, then simultaneously dip their heads and scoop up the concentrated fish with their bill pouches.

Date and Location Seen: _____

_____

Non-breeding

Immature

Description: 33", wingspan 52". Large, with **conspicuous bare yellow or orange skin on face and chin, thick neck**, relatively long wings. ADULT: **Black** head, neck, underparts; scaled above with gray and black. Bright orange-yellow skin in front of eyes and bare throat pouch. Breeding birds have white (or black and white) double crest plumes. IMMATURE: Varies from **brown to almost whitish on neck and breast**; belly darker; **bare face skin yellow**.

Similar Species: In flight, can be mistaken for geese, which are lighter-colored and have different flight. Common Loon (p. 71) is heavier, with thick, short neck and pointed bill.

Voice: Generally silent.

Where to Find: Locally common migrant (February-April, September-November) and summer resident of large marshes, lakes, creeks, and rivers, especially along the Columbia and Snake Rivers. Fairly common, but local winter resident along major ice-free creeks and rivers.

Behavior: Double-crested Cormorants pursue fish underwater; at surface they ride low in water with bill angled upward. Often seen perched on shore, rocks, or in trees with wings spread to dry. Forms colonies; builds stick nests in trees, often among nesting herons. Flocks commonly seen flying in "V" formations like geese.

Did you Know? This species is increasing throughout its range, aided by fish stocked in lakes and reservoirs.

Date and Location Seen: _____

_____

Description: 28", wingspan 42". Large, heavy-bodied wading bird with rich brown upperparts, **boldly streaked brown underparts**, a **black stripe on side of neck**, and green legs. **Dark flight feathers contrast with the brown upperparts** in flight.

Similar Species: Immature Black-crowned Night-Heron (p. 91) has blurry streaks on underparts, lacks black stripe on side of neck, and has rounder, even-colored wings.

Voice: Flight call is nasal *squark*; song is deep, repeating *LOONK-Aloonk*.

Where to Find: Uncommon and local summer resident (March-October) of low- to mid-elevation wetlands, rare in winter. Good locations include Camas N.W.R., Idaho; Ninepipe N.W.R., Montana; and Ladd Marsh W.M.A. and Buena Vista Ponds in Malheur N.W.R., Oregon.

Behavior: Forages for aquatic invertebrates and small vertebrates in wetlands with tall, emergent vegetation. Captures prey using stealth by standing motionless for long periods of time. Most active in early mornings and late evenings. Frequently calls at night during the breeding season. Shy and secretive, they hide from intruders by extending their necks and holding their bills pointed up in a reed-like pose.

Did you Know? This secretive and cryptically-plumaged marsh denizen can be remarkably difficult for birders to see; many more are heard in spring than are seen.

Date and Location Seen: _____

Adult

Description: 46", wingspan 72". Our **largest and most wide-spread heron**. Largely **gray**, with darker flight feathers. Has **cinnamon or chestnut "thigh" feathering**, strong, dagger-like bill that is mostly yellow, and grayish legs. ADULT: Has **whitish face, pale crown, long black head plumes**, and plain pale lavender-gray neck. JUVENILE: Has dark crown and much gray streaking on foreneck and breast.

Similar Species: Sandhill Crane (p. 123) flies with shallow wingbeats and an outstretched neck; has solid gray plumage with a red crown.

Voice: Calls are loud, deep and harsh, e.g. *RAAANK*.

Where to Find: Common summer resident, but concentrated near nesting colonies. Wanders widely after the breeding season. Winters near open water areas, mainly by larger creeks and rivers in low-elevation valleys.

Behavior: Patiently stalks shoreline or shallow water areas for fish, crayfish, frogs, and other prey. Also hunts mice in open fields during the winter. Often perches in trees. Nests colonially; builds large stick nests in tall, streamside trees. Flies with ponderous wingbeats, usually with neck folded in.

Did you Know? Studies conducted on the diet of Great Blue Herons in Idaho found that voles comprised nearly half of what the parent birds fed to their nestlings.

Date and Location Seen: _____

_____

**Great Egret
Adult**

**Snowy Egret
Breeding Adult**

Description: 39"/24", wingspan 51"/24". **All-white wading birds.** GREAT: **Large,** all white heron with very long slender neck, **yellow bill, black legs and feet.** Breeding adult has long plumes on the breast, lower back, rump. SNOWY: **Smaller,** with **slender black bill**; has mostly **black legs** that contrast with **yellow feet.** Skin between eyes and bill is deep yellow in adults. Breeding adult has white crest and long plumes on breast and rump.

Similar Species: Cattle Egret (rare, mostly in southeastern Idaho) much smaller and shorter-necked, with short yellow bill, blackish or orange legs and feet.

Voice: Both give harsh, grating calls.

Where to Find: GREAT: Fairly common but local summer resident (April-October) in southern portion of the region, occasionally nests. Uncommon in winter in southwest Idaho, rare elsewhere. SNOWY: Fairly common to rare and local summer resident (May-September) in southern portion of the region.

Behavior: Both species forage in shallow lakes, marshes, and upland meadows for fish and other small aquatic vertebrates, insects, and small terrestrial vertebrates. Great Egrets often nest in trees among Great Blue Heron colonies.

Did you Know? Populations of egrets were severely reduced by plume hunters in the late 1800s. This motivated preservationists to action and led to the establishment of what is now the National Audubon Society.

Date and Location Seen: _____

_____

Adult

Juvenile

Description: 25", wingspan 44". Medium-size, **stocky** heron with **short, thick neck** and red eyes. ADULT: **Black crown and back**, white forehead, gray wings, **pale gray underparts**. Bill is black, legs are yellow. Has one or two long, white head plumes. IMMATURE: Streaked gray-brown below, with white spots on the wings and small white streaks on the back. Legs are greenish to yellow, base of bill has much yellow.

Similar Species: Immature differs from American Bittern (p. 85) in grayer plumage tones, more uniform-colored wings, absence of black stripe below cheek.

Voice: Call is emphatic *quock*.

Where to Find: Resident of wetland habitats, including marshes, wooded streams, and swamps in low-elevation valleys. Fairly common in Oregon and Washington, uncommon and local in southern Idaho, and rare elsewhere. May be seen at McNary N.W.R. and Potholes Reservoir, Washington; Klamath Basin, Oregon; and Hagerman Wildlife Management Area, Idaho.

Behavior: Perches motionlessly at water's edge for long periods before striking fish, frogs, insects, mice, or other vertebrates and invertebrates. Usually nocturnal, forages most actively at dusk and dawn. During the day typically roosts in dense cover near water. Forms small to large breeding colonies, usually in trees.

Did you Know? Although not abundant in our region, this species is one of the world's most widespread species.

Date and Location Seen: _____

_____

Breeding Adult

Description: 23", wingspan 36". **Dark, glossy wading bird** with a **long, down-curved bill. Eyes are red, bill is gray**. BREEDING: Has glossy green back and wings with pink highlights; head, neck, and underparts are deep chestnut. **Bare pink skin on the face is surrounded by thin, white line of feathering**. NON-BREEDING: Has duller plumage with small white streaks on the neck, only a hint of white lines around limited pink on the face.

Similar Species: Glossy Ibis (very rare, but increasingly reported) is darker, lacks pink facial skin and red eyes, has white feathering both above and below the eye that does not meet.

Voice: Alarm call is low, quacking *waarr, waarr*.

Where to Find: Common summer resident (April-October) of southern Oregon and southeastern Idaho; rare, but increasingly reported elsewhere. Large numbers occur annually in Harney Basin, Oregon and at Camas N.W.R., Idaho.

Behavior: Feeds mainly on insects and other invertebrates. Gregarious, flies in close groups where large numbers occur. Feeds in flooded fields and shallow marshes. Nests colonially in extensive marshes. Semi-nomadic, they move to new feeding and nesting locations in response to seasonal drought or flooding.

Did you Know? Since the 1980s, the geographic range and numbers of White-faced Ibis expanded dramatically in our region, apparently in response to flooding of ibis colonies farther south.

Date and Location Seen: _____

_____

Adult

Description: 26", wingspan 66". Large raptor-like bird that is **blackish-brown** throughout, with a **bare reddish head** and whitish bill. The **flight feathers of the wings appear pale silvery from below**, contrasting with the darker body and wing linings. Appears small-headed in flight.

Similar Species: Golden Eagle (p. 99) has wings that appear more uniform in color from below, larger feathered head, and golden-brown hindneck.

Voice: Silent.

Where to Find: Common summer resident, migrant (March-April, September-October).

Behavior: Feeds on carrion, including road kills, which it locates by sight and smell. Travels long distances searching for food, soaring on slightly uptilted wings and often rocking back and forth in flight. Can be gregarious; gathers in late afternoon in tall trees to roost. Flocks of migrants ride thermal updrafts.

Did you Know? Turkey Vultures wait in the morning for updrafts to form before leaving their roost.

Date and Location Seen: _____

_____

Adult

Description: 23″. Large fish-eating hawk with a small, round head. Mostly **white on the head and underparts**, with a **dark mask through the eyes**, and a necklace of dark streaks across the breast; upperparts are blackish-brown. Juvenile is scaled with buff on the back and wings and has a buffy wash on the breast. Appears **gull-like in flight**, with wings angled and drooped slightly downward.

Similar Species: Bald Eagle (p. 99) is larger, stockier; lacks white underparts and dark tail.

Voice: Calls are short, chirping whistles.

Where to Find: Fairly common summer resident (March to October) along rivers and larger lakes; rare in winter.

Behavior: Forages by diving feet first into the water to capture fish, often hovering overhead before diving. Constructs large, bulky stick nests, usually constructed atop dead trees, utility poles, and man-made nest platforms.

Did you Know? After catching a large fish, an Osprey may flip the fish in mid-flight so that it is carried head first, before transporting it back to the bird's tree perch. Apparently they do this to make their flight more aerodynamic.

Date and Location Seen: _____

_____

Bald Eagle
Juvenile

Bald Eagle
Adult

Golden Eagle
Juvenile

Golden Eagle
Adult

Description: 31″/30″, wingspan 80″/79″. BALD: Adult has **dark brown body** with **white head and tail**. Immature is dark brown with variable white patches on body and wings. GOLDEN: Adult is **dark brown with golden crown and nape**, faintly banded tail. Immature has broad, white tail base, sometimes white wing patches.

Similar Species: Turkey Vulture (p. 95) has tiny, unfeathered head, holds its wings above horizontal while soaring, and has paler flight feathers.

Voice: Usually silent. Both species make weak, high-pitched calls.

Where to Find: BALD: Uncommon resident along rivers and large bodies of water. Largest wintering concentration in the lower 48 states is in Oregon's Klamath Basin. GOLDEN: Uncommon permanent resident of canyons, foothills, and mountains. Regular near Boise, Idaho.

Behavior: BALD: Forages mainly for fish plucked from the water's surface. Waterfowl and carrion are main food sources in winter. Builds large, bulky nests in trees. GOLDEN: Forages over open country for rabbits and other small vertebrates. Builds large, bulky nests in trees or on cliff ledges.

Did you Know? Bald Eagle populations were critically endangered by the 1940s, largely due to pesticide residues, ingestion of lead shot, and habitat loss. Since then, conservation efforts have brought about a remarkable recovery of their population.

Date and Location Seen: _____

_____

Female

Adult Male

Description: 18", wingspan 43". Long-winged, low-flying hawk with a banded tail; always shows a **conspicuous white rump** patch. Small head has owl-like facial disk. MALE: **Medium gray** head and upperparts; **whitish below** with some rusty spotting. Has **black wing tips**. FEMALE: Brown, with streaked underparts. JUVENILE: **Brown; pale rusty underparts** contrast with the dark head. In flight, holds wings slightly above horizontal.

Similar Species: Short-eared Owl (p. 191) has wider wings that are not held above horizontal in flight and lacks conspicuous white rump patch. Cooper's Hawk (p. 103) lacks facial disk and white rump patch.

Voice: Calls include high *eeya* and thin *sseeww*.

Where to Find: Common resident of open habitats in valleys. Numbers increase during migration (March-April, August-November), and often in winter.

Behavior: Forages for voles, small birds, and other vertebrates. Usually flies very low and buoyantly over the ground while hunting. Nests on the ground in a stand of tall grasses or other concealing vegetation. Highly nomadic species; population density is relative to prey abundance. Roosts communally on the ground in winter.

Did you Know? Research indicates that unlike other hawks, Northern Harriers rely on their acute sense of hearing as well as their keen vision to locate prey. Their low flights over the ground enable them to hear very small prey animals, such as voles.

Date and Location Seen: _____

_____

Sharp-shinned Hawk
Adult

Sharp-shinned Hawk
Juvenile

Cooper's Hawk
Adult

Cooper's Hawk
Juvenile

Description: 11"/16.5", wingspan 23"/31". Slender brown hawks with long, banded tails and short, rounded wings. SHARP-SHINNED: **Tail tip is squared**. Adult is **slate-gray above, barred with reddish below**. Juvenile is brown above, with some white spots; white underparts have rows of **teardrop-shaped reddish-brown spots**. COOPER'S: **Tail tip is rounded**. Adult has **blackish cap**, dark gray upperparts, reddish barring below; red eyes. Juvenile is brown above; rows of **thin, dark streaks** show on white underparts; has yellow eyes.

Similar Species: Larger Northern Goshawk (p. 105) has obvious white eyebrow.

Voice: SHARP-SHINNED: Call is high, thin series of *kew* notes. COOPER'S: Call is *kek kek kek kek* series.

Where to Find: Both are uncommon summer residents of deciduous, mixed, coniferous forests; fairly common in valleys during winter. Best observed in fall at the Lucky Peak hawk-watch near Boise, Idaho.

Behavior: Both feed mainly on small birds. Cooper's also takes small mammals. Hunt by making stealthy approach followed by short bursts of speed to capture prey. Usually build stick nests or refurbish old bird or squirrel nests. Both species are migratory; winter in valleys where small birds are plentiful. Patrol residential areas for birds at feeders.

Did you Know? Short, powerful, rounded wings and relatively long tails ensure Sharp-shinned and Cooper's Hawks speed, silent flight, and maneuverability in dense cover.

Date and Location Seen: _____

_____

Adult

Immature

Description: 21", wingspan 41". North America's largest accipiter. ADULT: **large, stocky hawk** with **thick, white eyebrow bordered by dark crown above and dark gray eye-line below; solid dark gray upperparts**, very pale gray breast with fine barring; white undertail, **long, indistinctly banded gray tail**; red eyes. IMMATURE: Speckled brown upperparts; underparts buffy with dense, dark brown streaking; head is pale brown with **bold white eyebrow**; tail unevenly banded dark brown and gray, undertail white with streaking; yellow eyes.

Similar Species: Smaller Cooper's Hawk (p. 103) lacks bold white eyebrow and undertail streaking. Gyrfalcon (rare) lacks bold white eyebrow and has longer, more pointed wings.

Voice: Call at nest is loud, strident *kye kye kye* series.

Where to Find: Uncommon and local summer resident of mature coniferous, mixed, or aspen forests. Uncommon and cyclic winter resident of valleys that have open areas interspersed with trees. Often winters at Boise and Deer Flat N.W.R., Idaho; Bennington Lake, Washington area; and McKay N.W.R., Oregon.

Behavior: Hunts by perching briefly and watching for prey. Feeds on birds and mammals, including grouse, squirrels, and rabbits. Prefers mature forests with large trees and open understories for nesting. Fiercely defends nest.

Did you Know? Northern Goshawks are well adapted for hunting in forests. Their short, powerful wings allow rapid acceleration, and long tail adds quick maneuverability between trees.

Date and Location Seen: _____

_____

**Adult
Light Morph**

**Adult
Dark Morph**

Description: 19", wingspan 51". Variably plumaged buteo with relatively slender, **pointed wings** and fairly long tail. Always has **dark breast and light undertail**. Often shows small whitish band on rump. ADULT: **White wing linings** contrast with dark flight feathers from below; has white chin, brown chest, and solid brown upperparts. Some adults are extensively rufous or dark brown below with rufous wing linings. JUVENILE: Mottled dusky and white; usually shows dark whisker mark and chest, pale chin; whitish or buffy wing linings are variably mottled with dusky.

Similar Species: Red-tailed Hawk (p. 109) has broader, blunter wings, a shorter, wider fan-shaped tail, and dark markings along leading edge of inner underwing.

Voice: Gives long, drawn-out *keeeeeah* scream on breeding territory.

Where to Find: Common summer resident of open, mostly treeless areas, common in spring (March-May) and fall migration (August-September).

Behavior: Buoyant flyer, sometimes catching large insects on the wing; also feeds on rodents and other small vertebrates. Migrants may gather into flocks of a hundred birds or more. Often nests in isolated tall trees in open areas.

Did you Know? Swainson's Hawks have a long journey to reach their wintering areas, with many travelling south as far as Argentina.

Date and Location Seen: _____

_____

Adult

Juvenile

Description: 19", wingspan 49". Most common and wide-spread large hawk. Bulky and broad-winged with a **broad tail**. Nearly always shows **pale mottling on the sides of the back**. ADULT: Usually with **reddish-orange tail**. Underparts vary from largely buffy with streaks across the belly to reddish brown or blackish. All but blackest birds show **distinct dark patch along the leading edge of the inner portion of the underwing**. JUVENILE: Most show some white on the breast, dark mottling on the belly, and have a finely-barred blackish and gray-brown tail. Many color morphs exist.

Similar Species: Ferruginous Hawk (p. 111) has a pale reddish tail but is much lighter overall. Swainson's Hawk (p. 107) has a small bill, relatively pointed wings, soars with wings raised above the horizontal, and lacks dark markings along the leading edge of the inner underwing.

Voice: Typical call is harsh, drawn-out scream; also gives shorter clipped notes.

Where to Find: Common permanent resident and migrant (March-April, September-November).

Behavior: Hunts ground squirrels and other small vertebrates, either from an elevated perch or by soaring overhead. Courting birds fly in tandem with legs dangled; they sometimes make long, aerobatic dives and rolls. Nests in trees or on cliffs.

Did you Know? This species was first described to science from the island of Jamaica, hence the name *jamaicensis*.

Date and Location Seen: _____

_____

Adult

Description: 23″, wingspan 56″. Our largest buteo hawk. ADULT: Gray and rufous above, **pure white below with dark rusty leggings** and dark-flecked flanks; Has **pale gray head, very pale tail**, large bill. JUVENILE: Like adult, but with dark brown upperparts, mostly white below, and faintly banded grayish tail.

Similar Species: Smaller Red-tailed Hawk (p. 109) has darker head, dark belly band, rufous tail (adults), and lacks dark leggings.

Voice: Gives a low-pitched whistle

Where to Find: Uncommon summer resident (February-October) of open rangeland. Rare in winter. Easily found near Fort Rock, Oregon; Red Rock Lakes N.W.R., Montana; and Snake River Birds of Prey National Conservation Area, Idaho.

Behavior: Mostly forages by soaring over and pouncing on ground squirrels and other small vertebrates. Also hunts from perches and spends considerable time on the ground. Nests on trees or cliff ledges, occasionally on the ground. Readily adopts manmade nest platforms and other structures. Shy, reacts negatively to disturbances.

Did you Know? Agricultural conversion of rangeland has seriously reduced Ferruginous Hawk populations.

Date and Location Seen: _____

_____

Light Morph

Immature Light Morph

Dark Morph

Description: 21", wingspan 53". Large buteo of open country with variable plumage. Commonly has a **white tail with a wide, black tip; pale, streaked breast; dark belly and pale head with a small bill**. In flight, **underwings** are **white with contrasting black wrist patches**. Soars with wings raised above the horizontal.

Similar Species: Red-tailed Hawk (p. 109) lacks prominent black wrist marks, white tail bases, and soars with wings held horizontally.

Voice: Usually silent.

Where to Find: Fairly common, but cyclic migrant and winter resident (October-May). Occupies open grassland areas in valleys, mainly rangeland, pastures, and marshes. Large numbers winter in the Mission Valley in western Montana most years.

Behavior: Primarily feeds on voles and other small rodents. Usually hunts from perch or by gliding low over the ground and dropping down on prey. Spends considerable time on the ground, but also uses higher perches. Usually found singly or in pairs, but will form large evening communal roosts in winter when prey densities are high.

Did you Know? The name "Rough-legged" refers to the birds' feathered legs; Rough-legged Hawks are one of only three American raptors with legs that are completely feathered.

Date and Location Seen: _____

_____

American Kestrel
Adult Male

American Kestrel
Female

Merlin Female

Merlin Male

Description: 10″/11″, wingspan 21″/23″. KESTREL: Small, **dainty** falcon with slender, pointed wings, long tail, and buoyant flight. Distinctive **black stripes on sides of white face**. Male has blue-gray wings, **rusty back, rusty tail** with black tip; buff below with black spotting. Female is larger, with barred rusty back, wings, and tail; underparts reddish streaked. MERLIN: **Small** but **powerfully built** falcon. **Tail usually banded black on gray**. Wings and back range from gray to sooty brown. Head has **white eyebrow** with no strong markings. Adult males are grayer above than females; all are **streaked below**.

Similar Species: Sharp-shinned Hawk (p. 103) has rounded wings, longer tail.

Voice: KESTREL: Call is series of shrill, rapid *kli* notes. MERLIN: Usually silent.

Where to Find: KESTREL: Common permanent resident of open country. MERLIN: Uncommon migrant and winter resident (September-April); rare breeder and summer resident in the northern portion of our region.

Behavior: Both species occur in open country. KESTREL: Perches on snags or posts and often hovers while hunting insects and small rodents in open meadows and fields. MERLIN: Favors sparse woodlands and brushy areas. Flies low and swiftly after birds and insects.

Did you Know? Both species regularly winter in suburban and urban areas, where they prey upon small vertebrates.

Date and Location Seen: _____

_____

Prairie Falcon Juvenile

Prairie Falcon Juvenile

Peregrine Falcon Adult

Peregrine Falcon Juvenile

Description: 16", wingspan 40". Swift, powerful, **crow-size falcons**. PRAIRIE: **Pale-brown above, white with brown streaks
or spots below. Flanks and "wingpits" blackish**; tail pale-
brown with faint bands. Brown head with white face and
throat, distinct brown "mustache mark", thin pale eyebrow,
and small gray bill. PEREGRINE: Adult **slate-gray above**, white
to creamy-buff underparts with **black barring on lower breast
and belly**. Tail gray with narrow black bars; underwing barred
with black. Juvenile is sooty-brown above, heavily streaked
below.

Similar Species: Larger Gyrfalcon (rare) has weak "mustache
mark".

Voice: PRAIRIE: Call is harsh *ree kree kree*. PEREGRINE: Call is
scolding *ray ray ray*.

Where to Find: PRAIRIE: Uncommon permanent resident of
open areas and cliff faces. PEREGRINE: Uncommon migrant
and rare, but increasing permanent resident. Both are seen at
Snake River Birds of Prey National Conservation Area near
Boise, Idaho; Ninepipe N.W.R., Montana; Walla Walla River
delta, Washington.

Behavior: PRAIRIE: Hunts over rangeland, pastures, and canyons
for small mammals, birds, and other small vertebrates. PER-
EGRINE: Mainly hunts for birds, including small waterfowl
and shorebirds. Both species nest on cliff ledges; Peregrines
also use high man-made structures.

Did you Know? Both species are among the fastest flying birds.

Date and Location Seen: _____

_____

Virginia Rail

Sora Adult

Description: 9.5"/8.75". VIRGINIA RAIL: Small, dark, short-tailed marsh bird that is usually well hidden. Has **long, thin, slightly down-curved red bill**. Adult has gray face, **bright rusty underparts** with **black and white vertical bars on flanks**. Feathers of upperparts are edged rusty. Immature is sooty. SORA: Plump marsh bird with **black face, stubby yellow bill**. Rusty-brown above, **gray below**. Immature is brown and buff, spotted with white.

Similar Species: Both are distinctive.

Voice: VIRGINIA RAIL: Male gives hard *gik gik gik gidik gidik gidik gidik* notes followed by accelerating series *wep wep-wepwepwepppprrr*. SORA: A rising *ko-WEE* followed by long, high squealing whinny; call is insect-like *keek*.

Where to Find: VIRGINIA RAIL: Common but secretive summer resident, uncommon in unfrozen marshes in winter. SORA: Common but secretive migrant and summer resident (March-October), rare in winter.

Behavior: Both walk through marsh vegetation, feeding mainly on aquatic invertebrates, small fish, and seeds. Sometimes feed more openly on mudflats, pond shores, but are usually shy and hidden. Flight appears weak and labored.

Did you Know? Rails are indeed "thin as a rail", having a narrow shape and flexible vertebrae adapted for maneuvering through reeds.

Date and Location Seen: _____

_____

119

Description: 15.5". Stocky, **dark-gray** aquatic bird with a **black head and neck**, and **chicken-like**, stout **white bill**. Small white streaks are on undertail sides; wings show white trailing edge in flight. Has small, dark red shield on forehead; thin, dark band near bill tip. Legs are greenish-yellow; **toes are lobed**. JUVENILE: Pale gray below; downy young have bright red head markings.

Similar Species: Pied-billed Grebe (p. 73) is colored plain, tawny-brown.

Voice: Call is clucking *kruk*.

Where to Find: Common migrant (April-May, September-October) and summer resident, fall concentrations often number in the thousands. Locally common in winter where open water exists, especially the lower Snake River and Columbia Basin.

Behavior: Dives and dabbles for aquatic plants and invertebrates, forages on mudflats, and grazes land adjacent to water. Flies reluctantly, pattering along water surface to get airborne; flight is rapid and a bit unsteady. Nests in marshes, and is aggressively territorial during breeding season.

Did you Know? Ducks sometimes pirate aquatic food plants from diving American Coots.

Date and Location Seen: _____

Adult

Description: 41-46", wingspan 73-77". Distinctive, tall, wading bird of open fields. **Very large**, with long neck and long legs. ADULT: **Entirely gray with red crown**, white cheek patch. Some summer birds stained rusty on body. Bill is dark. Long, drooping wing feathers cover short tail and form diagnostic "bustle". JUVENILE: All-gray with brownish wash on upperparts; lack red crown. Neck and legs fully extended in flight.

Similar Species: Smaller Great Blue Heron (p. 87) lacks red crown, has yellowish bill, flies with neck folded against body.

Voice: Call is loud, descending bugle-like roll.

Where to Find: Uncommon to rare and local summer resident. Common migrant (March-May, September-November), mainly along distinct flyways. Large numbers gather in spring at Malheur N.W.R., Oregon and near Othello, Washington.

Behavior: Omnivores, they forage in open grasslands, meadows, wetlands, and crop fields for plants, invertebrates, mice, and other small vertebrates. During breeding season, adults preen soil into their feathers, staining them rusty as a means of camouflage. Build large nests in open wet meadows and marshes where the birds have unlimited visibility. Congregate in large flocks in migration. Extremely wary, usually do not tolerate humans approaching them.

Did you Know? Sandhill Cranes perform elaborate and spectacular courtship displays. Paired birds face each other, bow, and then leap repeatedly into the air while calling with wings spread.

Date and Location Seen: _____

Breeding Adult
Male

Non-breeding

Description: 11.5". Large plover with a **stubby, black bill**. In flight, always shows **prominent white wing stripe, black "armpits", white rump** and undertail, and white tail with black barring. BREEDING: Black and white spotted back and wings, black face and breast with white border. NON-BREEDING: Brownish-gray upperparts, pale brownish streaked breast and flanks, and white belly. JUVENILE: Resembles winter adult but slightly browner and more neatly spotted with white above.

Similar Species: American Golden-Plover (rare) lacks black "armpits", pure white rump, white wing stripe.

Voice: High, plaintive whistle *plee-oo-EE*.

Where to Find: Uncommon to rare migrant (April-May, August-October), usually seen as singles or in small groups. Scarcer in spring than fall; most fall migrants in our region are juveniles. Regular at American Falls Reservoir and Mann Lake, Idaho; Pablo Reservoir and Ninepipe N.W.R., Montana; lower Columbia River Basin, Summer Lake, Malheur N.W.R. in Oregon; and Walla Walla River delta, Washington.

Behavior: Individuals in flocks spread out widely on mud flats and in plowed fields, usually avoiding each other while feeding. Feeds by sight, typically running short distances and then abruptly stopping to pick or probe for food.

Did you Know? Black-bellied Plovers are known as Grey Plovers in Great Britain, since they are mostly seen in drab grayish-brown non-breeding plumage.

Date and Location Seen: _____

_____

Killdeer

**Semipalmated Plover
Breeding Adult**

Description: 10.5"/7.25" KILLDEER: Familiar plover of upland and wetland habitats. Dark brown above with **orange rump and tail base**. Has white underparts with **two black breast bands**. In flight, appears long-tailed, and long wings show white stripe. SEMIPALMATED: Small plover with **dark brown back and complete breast band**. Bill is stubby; legs are yellow or orange. BREEDING: Face and breast band are black; bill has bright orange base. NON-BREEDING: Lacks black areas.

Similar Species: Snowy Plover (rare) paler with incomplete breast band.

Voice: KILLDEER: Very vociferous. Call is strident *deee, deeyee, tyeeeeeee deew deew, Tewddew*. SEMIPALMATED: Flight song is husky *too-ee, too-ee*; flight call is whistled *chu-WEE*.

Where to Find: KILLDEER: Common summer resident and migrant (February-November), uncommon and local in winter. SEMIPALMATED: Common migrant (April-May), July-September), rare in summer.

Behavior: Both forage using run-and-stop behavior to catch invertebrates on mudflats, shorelines. KILLDEER: Utilizes a variety of open habitats and nests on gravelly areas, including stream gravel bars and roadsides. Feigns broken wing to distract intruders approaching nest or young. Gregarious after the breeding season, large numbers gather at prime feeding locations, often with other shorebirds.

Did you Know? The Killdeer's buff and blackish-brown eggs are often virtually indistinguishable from their gravel surroundings.

Date and Location Seen: _____

_____

Black-necked Stilt
Male

Black-necked Stilt
Female

American Avocet
Breeding Female

American Avocet
Non-breeding Male

Description: 14"/18". STILT: Large, slender **black and white** shorebird with **extremely long pink to red legs. Bill is slender and straight**. Crown and hindneck are black, rump and underparts are white. Male's back is glossy black; breeding birds have buffy wash on breast. Female's back is washed with brown. AVOCET: Large **black and white shorebird** with **long, blue-gray legs** and **long, thin up-turned bill**. Has white back, black and white wings. **Head and neck** are a **rich tawny color** (breeding) or grayish (non-breeding).

Similar Species: Unmistakable. Differentiate these species on bill shape, head, neck, and leg color.

Voice: STILT: Call is loud, sharp *pleek*, often repeated. AVOCET: Call is high, sharp *kweep*.

Where to Find: STILT: Common summer resident (March-September) in the southern portion of the region, locally in Columbia Basin. They are rare but increasing elsewhere. AVOCET: Common summer resident (April-November), in the southern portion of the region, Columbia Basin, and northwestern Montana.

Behavior: STILT: Forages by picking and probing. AVOCETS: Feeds by sweeping curved bill back and forth beneath surface of water. Both species nest colonially and often together on open muddy edges of ponds and lakes.

Did you Know? Both species are very defensive at nest sites, mobbing approaching intruders with low intimidation flights and loud calls.

Date and Location Seen: _____

_____

Greater Yellowlegs
Breeding

Greater Yellowlegs
Juvenile

Lesser Yellowlegs
Breeding

Lesser Yellowlegs
Juvenile

Description: 14"/10.5". Both species have **long, bright yellow legs** and plain wings; also a mostly white rump and tail seen in flight. GREATER: Rather large shorebird with **long, slightly upturned bill that is gray at the base** (except in breeding plumage). Grayish with white spots above, pale below. In breeding plumage, heavily spotted and barred with blackish above and below. Juvenile has distinct streaks on breast. LESSER: Smaller, with **shorter and straighter bill that is always uniformly dark**. Plumage like Greater, but darker gray, especially on breast; less heavily marked in all plumages. Juvenile neck and breast are plainer gray.

Similar Species: Most likely to be confused with each other. Differentiate on bill characteristics and relative size. Smaller Solitary Sandpiper (rare) has prominent white eye-ring and shorter, greenish legs.

Voice: GREATER: Loud, shrill three-noted descending whistled *tew-tew-tew*. LESSER: Softer two-note *tu-tu*, often strung together in a series.

Where to Find: GREATER: Fairly common migrant (March-May, July-October). Uncommon to rare in winter, mainly along low-elevation, ice-free waters. LESSER: An uncommon spring (April-May), fairly common fall (July-October) migrant. Casual in winter.

Behavior: Both are active feeders, running about in shallow water to pursue small fish and aquatic invertebrates.

Did you Know? Greater Yellowlegs is one of our most cold-tolerant shorebirds.

Date and Location Seen: _____

Non-breeding

Description: 15". Stocky shorebird with a **striking black and white wing pattern in flight. Legs are gray; medium-length bill is gray, straight and fairly stout**. Plumage is **mostly gray**, becoming whitish on forehead and belly. BREEDING: Has barring and spotting on underparts, back and wings. JUVENILE: Neatly marked with small buff-white spots on back and wings. In flight, rump and tail are mostly white, wings show broad white stripe bordered by black.

Similar Species: Greater Yellowlegs (p. 131) has bright yellow legs.

Voice: Call is series of monotonous *wik* notes; song is *pill WILL WILLET*.

Where to Find: Common migrant and summer resident (April-September) in southern portion of our region north to central Idaho and Oregon. Rare migrant elsewhere.

Behavior: Forages mainly for aquatic insects and other invertebrates on mudflats and reservoir edges. Migrants stop at pond and lake margins, and freshwater marshes. Like many long-legged shorebirds, Willets quickly nod their heads up and down when alert, conspicuously call and fly over intruders near their nest sites.

Did you Know? Our western subspecies of Willet (*inornata*) differs from the eastern subspecies (*semipalmata*) in breeding plumage and size, and subtly in calls.

Date and Location Seen: _____

Breeding

Non-breeding

Description: 7.5". Distinctive shorebird that exhibits **constant bobbing, teetering motion**. NON-BREEDING: Brown above with white eyebrow. White below, with brownish patches on the sides of the breast. Bill is dark, legs are dull greenish-yellow or flesh-colored. Has broken white eye-ring. BREEDING: Thin dark bars above, **heavy black spotting below**; bill is extensively pink at the base; legs are pinkish-orange. Flies with stiff, shallow wingbeats.

Similar Species: Larger, darker Solitary Sandpiper (rare) has longer greenish legs, brownish breast, bold and complete white eye-ring; in flight shows dark underwings and black and white barred tail.

Voice: Call is high whistled notes *peet-weet*.

Where to Find: Common migrant and summer resident (April-September), rare in winter.

Behavior: Energetically walks pond, lake, or stream margins to forage, often lunging forward to grab insects. Usually seen in singles or in pairs, may occur in small, loose groups in migration. Distinctive flight consists of intermittent bursts of rapid, shallow wingbeats. Nests at all elevations along grassy edges of streams, ponds, and other water bodies.

Did you Know? Female Spotted Sandpipers may mate with up to four different males, leaving them to care for the eggs and chicks.

Date and Location Seen: _____

_____

Description: 23", wingspan 35". North America's largest shorebird. **Very large**, long-legged, with **long, slender, down-curved bill**. Upperparts mottled brown. Has plain crown; underparts buffy and subtly streaked; **underwings are bright cinnamon**; has pale gray legs. Immature has shorter bill and is paler.

Similar Species: Whimbrel (rare) has distinct head stripes, lacks cinnamon underwings, and has shorter down-curved bill. Marbled Godwit (p. 145) has long, straight or slightly up-curved bill and dark legs.

Voice: Call is loud rising *coooLI* and descending series of whistles.

Where to Find: Rare and local to fairly common migrant and summer resident (March-September) in most of the region. Mainly found in dry grasslands and pastures with short vegetation. Regular at Malheur N.W.R. and near Boardman in Oregon; Columbia N.W.R. in Washington; south of Kuna, Idaho; and Red Rock Lakes N.W.R. in Montana.

Behavior: Forages for grasshoppers and other invertebrates and small vertebrates in open, upland grasslands. Pairs perform aerial flight displays, and aggressively defend territories, nests, and young. Nest is on the ground and in the open, but well hidden and often adjacent to conspicuous objects, such as a rock or cow dung. Sometimes gathers in flocks at reservoirs in late summer during migration.

Did you Know? Female curlews are noticeably larger and longer-billed than the males.

Date and Location Seen: _____

_____

Western Sandpiper
Breeding

Western Sandpiper
Non-breeding

Least Sandpiper
Breeding

Least Sandpiper
Non-breeding

Description: 6.5"/6". WESTERN: **Blackish legs; relatively long bill with slight droop toward fine tip.** NON-BREEDING: Gray-brown above, whitish underneath. BREEDING: Variably rufous on crown, cheeks, and upperparts; breast, sides, flanks marked with dark arrow-shaped spots. JUVENILE: Cleanly marked gray and chestnut above, clean white below (breast is buffy in August). LEAST: The world's smallest sandpiper. Appears **short-winged** in flight; at rest the tips of the wings (primaries) are not visible on the folded wing. **Bill is short and very thin**, slightly arched. NON-BREEDING: **Gray-brown above, with brown wash across breast. Legs yellowish to dull greenish**. BREEDING: Breast strongly streaked; back feathers have black centers and some rufous fringes. JUVENILE: Rufous fringes to back and wing feathers, variable buffy wash across lightly streaked breast.

Similar Species: Semipalmated Sandpiper (uncommon to rare) has short, straight bill, black legs; juveniles lack rufous upperparts.

Voice: WESTERN: Call is high, scratchy *djeeet*. LEAST: Call is high trill *treep* or *tree-treep*.

Where to Find: Both highly gregarious and usually found together. Common migrants (April-May, July-October), rare in winter and summer.

Behavior: Both species forage on mudflats, picking and probing for small invertebrates. The more abundant Westerns often wade into shallow water to probe; the less numerous Leasts seldom wade.

Did you Know? The small *Calidris* sandpipers are collectively known as "peeps".

Date and Location Seen: _____

_____

Baird's Sandpiper
Juvenile

Pectoral Sandpiper
Juvenile

Description: 7.5"/8.75". BAIRD'S: Medium-size, **buffy sandpiper with very long wings**; stands with horizontal posture; has dark legs. JUVENILE: Gray-brown back and wings have buff-white fringes to feathers, yielding a **scaly appearance above. Breast is strongly washed with buff**, has short, dark streaks on the sides. Adults in breeding plumage are less scaly then juveniles, and have black spotting above. PECTORAL: Similar in structure, but larger than Baird's; **more patterned above, with strong band of streaks across breast; legs are yellowish.**

Similar Species: Smaller juvenile Least and Western Sandpipers (p. 139) lack Baird's distinct scaly appearance and very long wings. Pectoral Sandpiper similar to Least Sandpiper but much larger.

Voice: BAIRD's: Call is harsh, dry *kreeeel*. PECTORAL: Call is rich *churrk*.

Where to Find: Both are uncommon to rare spring (April-May) and uncommon-common fall migrants (July-September). Regular fall migrants at American Falls Reservoir, Idaho and Canyon Ferry Reservoir, Montana.

Behavior: Both feed slowly and deliberately on mudflats and in shallow water, but Baird's often feed well away from water and rarely venture into dense, marshy vegetation that Pectorals prefer.

Did you Know? In spring, most Baird's Sandpipers migrate north through the Great Plains. Pectorals mostly migrate north through the Mississippi and Ohio Valleys; they are among the world's longest-distance migrants.

Date and Location Seen: _____

Breeding

Non-breeding

Description: 8.5". Medium-size sandpiper with **long, drooping bill** and **blackish legs**. NON-BREEDING: Fairly dark and plain **gray-brown above** with pale brown head, faint whitish eyebrow, and **brown wash across breast**. BREEDING: Distinctive, with **rufous crown and back**, large **black belly patch**, streaked whitish face and breast.

Similar Species: Smaller Western Sandpiper (p. 139) is shorter-billed and cleaner white on breast. Baird's Sandpiper (p. 141) has shorter bill and longer wings.

Voice: Flight call is harsh *kreee*.

Where to Find: Uncommon spring migrant (April-May) in Oregon and Washington, rare in Idaho and Montana. Uncommon to rare fall migrant (September-November) throughout the region. Rare in winter with most sightings reported from the Columbia Basin, mainly at Walla Walla River and Yakima River deltas. Large numbers often stop at Summer Lake, Oregon in spring.

Behavior: Forages for invertebrates with other shorebirds at mudflats and shorelines. Often wades belly deep into shallow water, but also feeds on shore. Long bill enables it to forage deeper in mud or water than other small shorebirds.

Did you Know? North American Dunlins are among the few shorebirds that molt in the Arctic region after breeding. They arrive in our area relatively late in fall, already in their drab non-breeding plumage.

Date and Location Seen: _____

_____

Long-billed Dowitcher
Breeding

Long-billed Dowitcher
Non-breeding

Marbled Godwit
Adult

Description: 11.5"/18". DOWITCHER: Medium-size shorebird with **long, straight bill** and **triangular white patch on lower back. Tail finely-barred black and white**. NON-BREEDING: Grayish above and across breast, whitish belly. BREEDING: Upperparts mottled-black, buff, and rufous. White feather tips. Underparts chestnut-buff with **barring on sides of neck**. JUVENILE: Similar to non-breeding, but with buffy breast and rusty feather edges on upperparts. GODWIT: **Large, buffy-brown, long-legged** shorebird. Has **long, slightly up-curved bill with pinkish base, dark tip**. Shows **cinnamon-rufous** underwings in flight. Breeding birds have fine, dark barring on underparts.

Similar Species: Short-billed Dowitcher (rare) very similar to Long-billed Dowitcher, but gives rapid *tu-tu-tu* call. Larger Long-billed Curlew (p. 137) has large down-curved bill.

Voice: DOWITCHER: Sharp *keek*, often in rapid series. GODWIT: Common calls include hoarse *ke-RECK* and nasal *gowE-to gowEto gowEto*.

Where to Find: DOWITCHER: Common migrant (March-May, July-October), casual in winter. GODWIT: Fairly common migrant (April-May, July-September) to reservoirs and marshes in western Montana and southern Idaho. Rare elsewhere. Regular at American Falls Reservoir, Idaho and Ninepipe N.W.R., Montana.

Behavior: Both forage for aquatic invertebrates on mudflats by probing in mud with long bills.

Did you Know? Dowitchers employ a distinctive rapid "sewing-machine" probing motion to find invertebrates.

Date and Location Seen: _____

Adult

Description: 10.5". Stocky, brownish, short-legged shorebird with a **long, straight bill**. Crown and face are striped, and back has **long, creamy-white stripes**. Breast and flanks are barred with dusky, contrasting with white belly. **Orange tail** can be conspicuous when bird is flying away.

Similar Species: Long-billed Dowitcher (p. 145) has a white rump and longer legs; lacks pale head and back stripes.

Voice: When flushed, gives raspy *scaaip* call. Perched birds give loud display song *kit kit kit*. "Winnowing" males produce eerie low *huhuhuhuhuhuhuhuhuhu* whistled sounds during high overhead flights.

Where to Find: Common migrant and summer resident (March-October) of marshes. Rare and local in winter.

Behavior: Secretive, usually hiding motionlessly within short marshy vegetation; flushes with zig-zag flight, towering into the air, then dropping suddenly. Sometimes feeds more openly on mudflats, but rarely far from concealing vegetation. Usually found singly, but in good habitat small, loose groups may sometimes be found.

Did you Know? A male Wilson's Snipe produces "winnowing" sounds in flight high over a marsh to broadcast his intention to defend a territory and attract a mate. The sound is not produced by his voice, however, but by air flowing over thin, curved outer tail feathers.

Date and Location Seen: _____

_____

Breeding Female

Juvenile

Molting Juvenile

Description: 9.25". Phalaropes are unique swimming sandpipers with lobed toes; females are larger than males and much brighter in breeding plumage. Wilson's is a plump phalarope with **needle-like bill**. In flight, **wings are plain** and **rump is white**. BREEDING: Females have **broad dark-brown stripe through eye and down sides of neck**; hindneck is white and foreneck is apricot; males are similar but duller. NON-BREEDING: Pale grayish above, whitish below. Short greenish-yellow legs. JUVENILE: Dark feathering above has buffy edges; buff wash across front of neck in fresh plumage.

Similar Species: : Lesser Yellowlegs (p. 131) has longer legs, feeds by wading in shallow water. Smaller Red-necked Phalarope (p. 151) has short, needle-like bill, dark eye patch in non-breeding plumage, wing stripes, dark centered tail.

Voice: Call is low, grunting *wemp*, often given in short series.

Where to Find: Common migrant and summer resident (April-September). Most move to key staging areas in July and August, e.g. Lake Abert and other south central Oregon alkaline lakes.

Behavior: Swims, spinning rapidly to bring food to surface on shallow marshes or marshy edges of lakes. More likely seen feeding on mudflats then other phalaropes, walking with forward-lunging gait, picking up brine flies, other prey.

Did you Know? In fall, Wilson's Phalaropes migrate to wetlands in South America, some traveling as far south as Tierra del Fuego.

Date and Location Seen: _____

_____

Breeding Female

Juvenile

Description: 7.75". Our smallest phalarope, with a **short, thin bill**, white **wing stripes**, and dark central tail feathers. NON-BREEDING: Has **dark patch through the eye; back striped** dark gray and white. BREEDING: Has slaty crown and face, white patch on sides of throat, red neck sides; sides of breast dark gray, upperparts gray with gold stripes. Females are darker and brighter than males. JUVENILE: Like non-breeding adult, but with dark cap, black and buff upperparts.

Similar Species: Larger Wilson's Phalarope (p. 149) has a prominent white rump. Larger non-breeding Red Phalarope (rare) is pale gray and white with a heavier bill.

Voice: Call is hard *kett*.

Where to Find: Uncommon to fairly common migrant (April-May, July-September) with largest numbers staging at alkaline lakes. Major migration stops in our region include Lake Abert, Oregon and Walla Walla River delta, Washington.

Behavior: Forages for insects during the breeding season and when on fresh water; also feeds on brine shrimp at saline lakes, and zooplankton and other small creatures when at sea. Highly social, often forms post-breeding flocks.

Did you Know? Red-necked Phalaropes often feed by spinning rapidly in tight circles to create upwellings that bring small food items to the water's surface.

Date and Location Seen: _____

_____

Franklin's Gull
Breeding Adult

Franklin's Gull
Non-breeding

Bonaparte's Gull
Breeding Adult

Bonaparte's Gull
Immature

Description: 14.5"/13.5", wingspan 36"/33". FRANKLIN'S: **Small hooded gull**. BREEDING: **Head is black** with **prominent white eye-arcs** joined only at rear; has red bill. Upperparts ashy gray, wings are gray with white trailing edge and **white-spotted, black wingtips**; underparts are entirely white, **bill is blood-red colored with a fine, dark subterminal band**. BONAPARTE'S: **Small**, tern-like gull with **slender black bill**, pink legs. NON-BREEDING: Pale gray above with white head; **black spot is behind eye**. Has white underparts. **White triangle on outer wing is bordered behind by black**. BREEDING: **Head is black**.

Similar Species: Smaller Little Gull (rare) adults have black underwings.

Voice: FRANKLIN'S: Short, hollow *kowii*. BONAPARTE'S: Low, grating *gerrrr*.

Where to Find: FRANKLIN'S: Common summer resident of southeast Idaho and Malheur N.W.R., Oregon. Uncommon to rare transient elsewhere. BONAPARTE'S: Uncommon to fairly common migrant (April-May, September-November), rare in winter. Large flocks gather in fall at Klamath Falls, Oregon and American Falls, Idaho.

Behavior: FRANKLIN'S: Sociable. Walks plowed farm fields in huge numbers or swims in marshes and other water bodies. Forages for insects, earthworms, and small vertebrates. Nests in marshes. BONAPARTE'S: Plucks small fish or invertebrates from surface of water or plunge dives to capture prey.

Did you Know? Bonaparte's Gulls nest in trees near water in Alaska and Canada.

Date and Location Seen: _____

_____

**Ring-billed Gull
Breeding Adult**

**Ring-billed Gull
Non-breeding Adult**

**California Gull
Breeding Adult**

**California Gull
Non-breeding**

Description: 17.5"/21", wingspan 46"/53". Medium-size gulls with pale gray back and wings, black wingtips with white spots, white head and underparts, yellow bill, and **yellowish legs**. RING-BILLED: Breeding adult has **black ring near bill tip and yellowish-white eye**. Non-breeding adult has head and neck flecked with brown. CALIFORNIA: Adult similar to Ring-billed, but **larger**. Upperparts **slightly darker gray, eyes dark, bill yellow with red and black spots near tip**. Non-breeding adult has head and chest streaked with brown.

Similar Species: Adult Mew Gull (rare) similar to Ring-billed, but lacks distinct, black ring at or near tip of its shorter, more slender bill, and has larger white spots on its outer wingtips.

Voice: Both give high, hoarse cries.

Where to Find: RING-BILLED: Common summer resident and migrant (February-November), common in winter in open water areas. CALIFORNIA: Common summer resident and migrant (March-September). Common to rare in winter.

Behavior: Both species feed, rest, and roost together. Omnivorous, they forage in farm fields, on bodies of water, landfills, parks, dams, and residential areas for invertebrates, small vertebrates, and refuse. Typically make dawn and dusk flights between communal roosts and feeding locations. Often breed near each other on islands.

Did you Know? Like most gulls, Ring-billed and California Gulls are opportunistic feeders, eating anything they can catch or scavenge.

Date and Location Seen: _____

_____

Non-breeding Adult

First-year

Description: 25", wingspan 58". Large pink-legged gull with a long, fairly thin bill. ADULT: **Upperparts are pale gray, with limited black in the wingtips. Eyes are pale yellowish, legs are bright pink.** In winter, adults are streaked and mottled with brown on the head and neck. IMMATURE: Variable. First-year birds are mottled brown, with the head often noticeably paler. The mantle becomes increasingly gray and underparts become whiter through the second and third years. On flying immatures, note that flight feathers are paler toward mid-wing than at the tip.

Similar Species: Smaller California Gull (p. 155) is slimmer and adults have greenish legs. Very similar Thayer's Gull (rare) is smaller and more delicately built, with a smaller bill and dark eyes.

Voice: Typical gull squeals and cackles.

Where to Find: Common migrant and winter resident (September-May) along the Columbia and Snake Rivers and in Oregon's Klamath Basin. Uncommon migrant (February-May, September-November). Rare elsewhere in winter.

Behavior: Forages mainly for fish with other gull species at reservoirs and rivers, and for urban refuse at landfills. Joins other gulls in large winter roost flights.

Did you Know? Herring Gulls are the most common and widespread gull in North America.

Date and Location Seen: _____

_____

Non-breeding Adult

First-year

GLAUCOUS-WINGED GULL
Larus glaucescens

Description: 26", wingspan 58". **Large** and stocky Pacific Coast gull with a gray back and wings; white head, tail, and underparts. Has **pink legs, dark eyes**, and a long, heavy yellow bill with a red spot. NON-BREEDING: Adult has **extensive pale brownish mottling on head and neck, unicolored light gray back and wings**. First-winter immature is **mottled pale grayish-brown throughout** with an all-black bill.

Similar Species: Adult Western Gull (rare) has white head, dark gray back and black wingtips, and robust bill thickened at tip. Smaller Herring Gull (p. 157) has pale gray upperparts and black wingtips.

Voice: Typical gull calls.

Where to Find: Uncommon migrant and winter resident (October-April) along the lower Columbia (where it is a locally rare breeder) and Snake Rivers. Rare elsewhere in the region. Annual in southwestern Idaho and at Flathead Lake, Montana.

Behavior: Forages on large rivers, reservoirs, and landfills for anything edible. Typically seen with other gulls in massive winter flocks at reliable feeding locations.

Did you Know? Glaucous-winged and Western Gulls commonly interbreed.

Date and Location Seen: _____

Breeding Adult

Description: 21", wingspan 48". Our largest tern. Has a stout, **deep red bill** and tail slightly forked. Always has **blackish underneath the wingtips**. Breeding adult has a black crown, squared at the rear. Upperparts are pale gray, otherwise white. Legs are black.

Similar Species: All other terns are much smaller.

Voice: Call is deep, harsh *kraa-aay-ow*.

Where to Find: Common migrant and summer resident (March-September), mainly along the Columbia and Snake Rivers and the southern portion of our region. Rare elsewhere.

Behavior: Makes low foraging flights over water for fish, plunges into water to make catch. Breeds in colonies on islands with, but apart from California and Ring-billed Gulls. Often stands on river bars, mudflats, or lakeshores when not feeding. Frequently wanders in search of reliable food sources after breeding.

Did you Know? Caspian Terns are the largest, most aggressive, and least gregarious of our terns.

Date and Location Seen: _____

_____

Forster's Tern
Breeding Adult

Forster's Tern
First winter

Common Tern
Breeding Adult

Common Tern
Immature

Description: 13"/12", wingspan 31"/30". Medium-size terns with pale gray upperparts, black crowns (breeding), long, deeply forked white tails. FORSTER'S: Breeding adult has **orange bill** with dark tip, **orange legs, silvery-white wings**. Non-breeding adults and immatures have **white crown, black patch extending back from eye**, darker flight feathers, black bill. COMMON: Breeding adult has **red bill** with dark tip, **red legs**, pale gray underparts, **gray wings with black wedge on trailing edge**. Non-breeding adults and immatures have **black rear hood**, black or mostly black bill and legs, **dark bar at bend of wing**.

Similar Species: Larger Caspian Tern (p. 161) has thick, red bill.

Voice: FORSTER'S: Call is descending *kerrr*. COMMON: Call is harsh *kee-arrr*.

Where to Find: FORSTER'S: Common migrant, locally common summer resident (April-September). Nests mainly in southern portion of our region and Columbia Basin, uncommon elsewhere. COMMON: Uncommon fall migrant (August-October), rare in spring and summer. Found mainly along the Columbia and Snake Rivers. Concentrations occur at Walla Walla River delta, Washington; McNary Dam, Oregon; and American Falls Reservoir, Idaho.

Behavior: Both forage for small fish, nest colonially. FORSTER'S: Nests in open-water marshes. COMMON: Nests on islands. Both regularly visit Columbia and Snake River dams in fall.

Did you Know? Tern populations were devastated by the millinery trade in the late 19th century.

Date and Location Seen: _____

_____

Breeding Adult

Juvenile

Description: 9.75", wingspan 24". Small, dark, short-tailed tern. All plumages have **gray wings, underwings**, back, and tail. Undertail is white, bill is thin and black. BREEDING: Has mostly **black body**. NON-BREEDING: Adult and immature have white heads with black crown and ear patches, underparts white with dark patches on sides of breast.

Similar Species: All other terns have white underwings, pale gray backs, and are larger.

Voice: Call is harsh *keff*.

Where to Find: Common migrant and locally common summer resident (April-September). Large numbers regularly nest at Turnbull N.W.R. and Okanogan Highland lakes, Washington; Malheur N.W.R. and Klamath Basin, Oregon. Disperses in migration with no obvious concentrations.

Behavior: Diet is mainly insects and other aquatic invertebrates, and small fish. Feeds with buoyant, erratic flight. Flocks swoop to pluck prey from water's surface or by catching insects on the wing. Breeds colonially in wetlands that have dense emergent vegetation and open water areas.

Did you Know? Black Tern populations have declined in many areas due to the loss of wetland habitats.

Date and Location Seen: _____

_____

Description: 13". Quintessential domestic bird of cities and other areas of human habitation. "Wild type" birds are mainly gray with **white rump band, black wing-bars, white wing linings**, and iridescent neck sides; tail has black terminal band and white edges. Bill is black and legs are pink. An **array of other plumages** is noted in city flocks, from pure white to reddish brown or nearly black; many are pied and asymmetrically marked.

Similar Species: Larger Band-tailed Pigeon (rare) has orange-yellow bill and feet, white hindneck crescent and uniform gray plumage with darker flight feathers.

Voice: Gruff cooing notes; wings often make clapping sound on take-off.

Where to Find: Common resident of cities and agricultural areas. Colonies often located in canyons or on rock outcrops.

Behavior: Abundant, tame, and ubiquitous. Forages for grain and seeds in farm fields, along roads, and in cities. Introduced species that nests colonially on cliff faces, usually near agricultural areas where it feeds. In cities and towns or around farms it nests on ledges of buildings or bridges, and other tall structures. Typically remains in flocks throughout the year.

Did you Know? Rock Pigeons have been associated with humans for thousands of years.

Date and Location Seen: _____

_____

Mourning Dove

Eurasian Collared-Dove

Description: 12"/13". MOURNING: Slender pale brown dove with **pointed, white-edged tail**, black facial spot, and a few **black spots on the wings**. Legs are pink, eye-ring is pale bluish. COLLARED-DOVE: Pale gray-brown with **black hindneck collar** and **dark wingtips**. Has long, broad, **square tail with dark gray base** and white corners, and **gray undertail coverts**.

Similar Species: Ringed Turtle-Dove (a.k.a. African Collared-Dove) is a frequently escaped cage bird and smaller, paler version of Eurasian Collared-Dove that lacks dark wingtips and undertail.

Voice: MOURNING: Mournful *ooAAH coooo coo coo*. COLLARED-DOVE: Three-syllable hooting *coo COOO cup*.

Where to Find: MOURNING: Common migrant and summer resident. Does not occur in heavily wooded areas and is most common in agricultural and suburban areas. Locally common in winter along the Columbia and Snake Rivers, rare elsewhere. COLLARED-DOVE: Local resident of some agricultural and residential areas; population and geographic extent are rapidly expanding.

Behavior: Both forage for seeds on the ground in open habitats. Commonly seen on overhead wires. Except when nesting, both species are gregarious, and form wintering flocks that visit feedlots and farm fields.

Did you Know? Although Mourning Doves suffer substantial losses of nests and young, they maintain very high population levels by nesting several times a year.

Date and Location Seen: _____

_____

Description: 16″, wingspan 42″. Medium-size, very **pale buffy, gray and white** owl with **dark eyes** and **heart-shaped face**. FEMALE: Usually deep buff on underparts. MALE: Underparts all-white. Large rounded head with no ear-tufts. Appears entirely white at night when flying overhead.

Similar Species: Short-eared owls (p. 191) have dark wing patches, distinctly barred breasts, and moth-like flight.

Voice: Common call is rasping screech, often given in flight.

Where to Find: Fairly common resident of open, low-elevation areas. Rare in northern Idaho and Montana.

Behavior: Active at night, hunts for rodents with long, coursing flights. Roosts quietly during the day in trees, cut banks, or structures (barns and outbuildings, haystacks, bridges). Nests in large tree cavities, cut banks, ledges, old buildings, haystacks, or suitably large nest boxes. Breeding cycle dependant upon prey numbers; can breed any time of year. Incurs major losses from vehicles on highways, especially in southern Idaho.

Did you Know? Barn Owls have exceptionally keen hearing and can locate rodents and other prey in total darkness.

Date and Location Seen: _____

_____

Description: 6.75". Very small, migratory, **dark-eyed** forest owl. Overall mottled gray with **pale, dark, and cinnamon highlights**; has **short ear tufts** (often not visible) and a **round, gray or rusty facial disk**.

Similar Species: Larger Western Screech-Owl (p. 175) has yellow eyes.

Voice: Song is low, soft *boop* or *bodo-boop* hoots in series.

Where to Find: Uncommon summer resident of dry, open coniferous and mixed forests, rare migrant (May-June, August-October) elsewhere in our region. Good locations include the Nez Perce National Forest, Idaho; Lolo National Forest, Montana; Malheur National Forest, Oregon; and Blewett Pass and Okanogan Highlands, Washington.

Behavior: Forages mainly for crickets, moths, beetles, and other insects. Most active just before dark and just before dawn. Mostly gleans insects from foliage, but also catches prey in mid-air or on the ground. Mainly nests in cavities, usually uses old woodpecker nest holes.

Did you Know? The low, soft, ventriloquil toots of Flammulated Owls often make them very difficult for birders to locate.

Date and Location Seen: _____

_____

Description: 8.5". Small, finely-marked **grayish** woodland owl with **yellow eyes**, short "ear" tufts (often not visible), **white spots on sides of back and wings**. Like most of our owls, it is best detected and identified by voice.

Similar Species: Smaller Flammulated Owl (p. 173) has dark eyes. Northern Saw-Whet Owl (p. 193) lacks "ear" tufts, has coarsely streaked underparts.

Voice: Calls include barking, chuckling; song is an accelerating "bouncing ball" series of short, low whistles *hoo hoo hoo-hoo-hoo-oo-oo-oo-oo*.

Where to Find: Uncommon resident of riparian woodlands, parks and urban areas with large, mature deciduous trees.

Behavior: Omnivorous, they perch in likely areas and wait for prey consisting of small rodents, birds and many other vertebrates. Also consume moths, crickets, crayfish and other invertebrates. Nest in tree cavities or man-made nest boxes. Nocturnal, they generally occupy daytime roosts in snags, dense shrub or tree cover, or in outbuildings.

Did you Know? To find Western Screech-Owls, walk quietly through mature cottonwood riparian forests at night in the spring or early summer while listening for their characteristic "bouncing ball" song.

Date and Location Seen: _____

_____

Description: 22", wingspan 44". Our familiar **large, tufted** owl. The size of a Red-tailed Hawk, with **yellow eyes**, finely-barred and streaked brown, gray and white plumage. Has conspicuous **white throat** collar. Females are larger than males.

Similar Species: Smaller Long-eared Owl (p. 189) has longer and more closely-spaced "ear" tufts and more streaked underparts.

Voice: Song is familiar, deep *hoo h'HOOO hoo hoo*. Juvenile begging call is eerie, rasping *reeeek*.

Where to Find: Common resident of semi-open, low- to mid-elevation areas in almost all habitats in the region, including residential areas with parks and woodlots.

Behavior: Typically hunts at night from perches overlooking open areas. Diet is usually rodents, but can include many other small or medium-size vertebrates, such as rabbits, skunks, and smaller owls. Calling birds often sit conspicuously atop tall trees and utility poles. Nest sites include old stick nests built by other large birds, broken snag tops, cliff face ledges, and buildings.

Did you Know? Great Horned Owls are surprisingly early breeders, often initiating courtship and nesting in winter.

Date and Location Seen: _____

_____

Description: 23", wingspan 52". **Large** nomadic, mostly **white owl** with yellow eyes, pure white face, and round head lacking "ear" tufts. MALE: Body is mostly white with faint dark markings throughout. FEMALE, IMMATURE: Heavily barred with black on white.

Similar Species: Much smaller Barn Owl (p. 171) can appear white (especially when seen flying overhead), but is tawny brown on upperparts.

Voice: Mostly silent.

Where to Find: Rare and irregular winter visitor from the Arctic, most often seen in open areas, e.g. fields, roadsides, airports. Best locations are usually Montana's Flathead and Mission Valleys, and Washington's northern Lincoln County and Potholes Reservoir area.

Behavior: Opportunistic hunters, they perch on the ground, fence posts, and buildings watching for voles and other small vertebrate prey. They hunt by day or night, but prefer low light conditions. Occasionally take larger prey, including grebes, ducks, and rabbits.

Did you Know? In winters with poor lemming populations in the Arctic, small numbers of Snowy Owls "irrupt" or migrate to our region in search of food.

Date and Location Seen: _____

_____

179

Description: 6.75". **Small, long-tailed owl with yellow eyes**. The head is brown with tiny white spots, and **back of its head has two black false "eye-spots" outlined in white**. Upperparts are grayish-brown with pale spots; belly is white with narrow, dark streaking; breast and sides are grayish-brown with tiny white spots, and the tail is narrowly barred dark and white.

Similar Species: Northern Saw-whet Owl (p. 193) has shorter tail. Larger Western Screech-Owl (p. 175) has ear tufts.

Voice: Song is series of repeated single or double toots, often following low, rapid series, as in *popopopopopo, too, too, too*.

Where to Find: Uncommon resident of coniferous and mixed forests. Prefers areas with scattered openings rather than large tracts of unbroken forest.

Behavior: Hunts primarily at dawn and dusk, though often seen in daytime. Forages for rodents, large insects, and small birds. A swift and aggressive hunter, it readily chases birds in flight or small mammals running on the ground. Nests in natural tree cavities or old woodpecker holes. Commonly makes altitudinal migrations to lower elevations in fall and winter, usually following prey.

Did you Know? Northern Pygmy-Owls sometimes kill birds and mammals larger than themselves

Date and Location Seen: _____

_____

Description: 9.5". Small, **long-legged**, tuft-less owl of open country. The **yellow eyes**, broad white chin, and **white "eyebrows"** are distinctive. Body plumage is spotted and barred, brown and white. IMMATURE: Has buffy, unmarked underparts.

Similar Species: Much larger Short-eared Owl (p. 191) has boldly-streaked underparts.

Voice: Rasping, rapid barking series *kwik-kwik-kwik*.

Where to Find: Uncommon to rare and local summer resident (March-September) of sparsely vegetated open rangelands and pastures, mainly in the Columbia Basin, southeastern Oregon, and southern Idaho. Breeds in Snake River Birds of Prey National Conservation Area, south of Boise, Idaho.

Behavior: Forages for small invertebrates and vertebrates. Active in daytime, perching on low elevated outposts near nest burrow while watching for prey. Perched bird bobs up and down when agitated. Nests in abandoned animal burrows or artificial holes in the ground. Flight is low, with quick flaps and a glide, sometimes hovers.

Did you Know? Burrowing Owls place animal dung in and around their burrows. One theory is that the dung masks the birds' scent from predators, such as coyotes or badgers.

Date and Location Seen: _____

_____

Description: 21″, wingspan 42″. **Medium-size**, stocky, **round-headed forest owl** with **dark eyes** and **no ear-tufts**. Upper-parts are brownish with pale spots and bars, head is paler. Underparts are whitish with horizontal barring on throat, has **bold vertical brown barring** below, yellowish bill.

Similar Species: Larger Great Gray Owl (p. 187) has yellow eyes, distinctive "bowtie" marking.

Voice: Call is distinctive *hoo hoo wa-hoo, hoo hoo wa-hoo-aaaaah* ("who cooks for you, who cooks for you all").

Where to Find: Uncommon and local resident of forests. Sometimes winters in residential parks and woodlots. Population apparently increasing.

Behavior: Forages for mammals, birds and other vertebrates, and large invertebrates. Hunts by sitting in wait for prey, then silently swooping down to make capture. Mainly forages at night and roosts during the day in concealing vegetation. Nests in tree cavities and on abandoned nests of other large birds or squirrels. Typically does not flush when approached, but remains still and hidden.

Did you Know? Barred Owl is an eastern North American species that has spread north and westward through Canada, first reaching our region about the early to mid-1920s in northwestern Montana.

Date and Location Seen: _____

_____

Description: 27", wingspan 52". **Very large** owl with **massive, round head without ear tufts and small yellow eyes. Mottled grayish pattern overall**; face is outlined by **large, gray facial disc**, prominent **black and white "bowtie"** marking on throat. Wings are broad, tail is long and faintly banded.

Similar Species: Smaller Barred Owl (p. 185) has dark eyes and lacks distinctive white "bowtie" marking.

Voice: Low, labored *hoooaah* hoots in long series.

Where to Find: Rare and local resident of mature coniferous forests adjacent to wet meadows or pastures. Locations include Red Rock Lakes N.W.R., Montana; Targhee National Forest, Idaho; Spring Creek and Fort Klamath areas in Oregon, and northern Blue Mountains of Washington.

Behavior: Forages by sitting and waiting for prey or by making low reconnaissance flights for voles, pocket gophers, and mice. Hunts by day or night. Often plunges through several inches of snow for rodents detected by sensitive hearing. Uses old stick nests of other large birds, broken off snag tops, or man-made nesting platforms for nests. Makes altitudinal migrations in winter in response to food availability. Forms loose groups in winter where prey numbers are especially plentiful.

Did you Know? Great Gray Owl is the longest North American owl with the largest wingspan, but is easily outweighed by both Great Horned and Snowy Owls.

Date and Location Seen: _____

_____

Description: 15″, wingspan 36″. **Medium-size**, slender owl with **yellow eyes, long, closely-spaced "ear" tufts, and tawny-orange facial disc**. Upperparts are gray, underparts are mottled brown with black **vertical streaking and barring**. In flight, large tawny-orange patches are visible on outer wings, and prominent black patches near "wrist".

Similar Species: Larger Great Horned Owl (p. 177) has horizontal barring on underparts, widely spaced "ear" tufts. Short-eared Owl (p. 191) lacks long "ear" tufts, barred underparts, and is paler.

Voice: Male gives low, soft *wooip*. Both sexes produce soft barks, squeals, and mewing calls.

Where to Find: Uncommon and local residents of riparian woodlands, planted treebelts, Russian olive thickets, and open coniferous forests, especially near water and adjacent to open areas.

Behavior: Forages at night for small mammals in open areas and roosts by day in thickets. Typically utilizes abandoned stick nests of Black-billed Magpies, American Crows, and hawks for nesting. Forms communal roosts in winter, usually in thickets adjacent to open lowland areas.

Did you Know? Like some other owls, Long-eared Owls have asymmetrical ear openings which help them locate prey by sound.

Date and Location Seen: _____

_____

Description: 15", wingspan 38". **Medium-size owl of open country with round head and yellow eyes.** Short "ear" tufts not usually visible. **Flight is buoyant**, moth-like. Upperparts are mottled brown, underparts are pale with fine streaking. Eyes are surrounded by dark patches. Large **buff patches on outer wings** and **prominent black patches near "wrist"** show in flight.

Similar Species: Female Northern Harrier (p. 101) has smaller head, long tail, darker upperparts, and less buoyant flight. Long-eared Owl (p. 189) has long "ear" tufts, rusty facial disc, buffy underwings, smaller wrist patch, and darker belly.

Voice: Calls include nasal barks and wheezy notes. Male gives rapid *poo-poo-poo-poo-poo* series and claps its wings together during breeding display flight.

Where to Find: Uncommon to rare and local, and declining resident and migrant (March-April, October-November) in lowland grasslands, marshes, and wet meadows. Abundance is highly variable from year to year, depending upon prey population cycles. Fairly regular at Ted Trueblood W.M.A., Idaho; Ninepipe N.W.R., Montana; Malheur N.W.R., Oregon.

Behavior: Forages both day and night, mainly for small rodents. Typically flies low over the ground and pounces on prey. Nests and roosts on the ground. Nomadic in times of prey scarcity.

Did you Know? Short-eared Owls perform spectacular courtship displays, where males fly high into the air above perched females while hooting and rapidly clapping their wings.

Date and Location Seen: _____

_____

Juvenile

Description: 8″. Small, **round-headed, yellow-eyed** owl. Upperparts brown with white spots on the wings; underparts are white with broad, brown streaks; **face and head have fine, white streaks**; has short tail.

Similar Species: Boreal Owl (rare) is larger, has yellow bill, black outline to face. Northern Pygmy-Owl (p. 181) is diurnal, has longer tail and false "eye-spots" on the back of the head. Larger Western Screech-Owl (p. 175) is darker and has ear tufts.

Voice: Song is rhythmic series of low, whistled *poo poo poo* notes repeated rapidly. Other vocalizations may include screeches and soft barks.

Where to Find: Uncommon to fairly common, but secretive resident of forest habitats. Population densities are highest in mid-elevation coniferous forests.

Behavior: Nocturnal, often remains well hidden in dense cover (usually in conifers) during the day. Hunts at night from low perches. Nests in woodpecker holes or natural cavities, but readily uses nest boxes. Occasionally migrates southward or down slope in the fall, sometimes in great numbers.

Did you Know? Northern Saw-whet Owls are small mammal specialists; they especially prey upon deer mice.

Date and Location Seen: _____

Common Nighthawk

Common Poorwill

Common Nighthawk

Description: 9.5"/7.75". NIGHTHAWK: Grayish-brown above, banded brown below; long, narrow **wings with white bands** near wingtips; long, notched tail. Flies with erratic, deep wingbeats, gliding on raised wings. POORWILL: Small, mottled-brown bird with **large, flat-topped head and short, rounded wings and tail**. Throat black with white band below. **White** (male) or **buffy** (female) **tail corners**. Flight is floppy and moth-like.

Similar Species: When perched, owls look similar but have facial discs and perch vertically.

Voice: NIGHTHAWK: Call is loud, nasal *SPEEK SPEEK*, and loud, whooshing *Hooov* produced by display dives of males. POORWILL: Call is low *poorWillip*.

Where to Find: NIGHTHAWK: Common migrant (May-June, August-September) and summer resident in open areas. POORWILL: Fairly common migrant and summer resident (April-October) in dry, open, shrubby areas with rocky ledges, often in canyons.

Behavior: Both species capture flying insects on the wing. NIGHTHAWK: Makes long foraging flights at dusk, night, and on overcast days. POORWILL: Flies from the ground to capture insects flying overhead. Both roost on bare ground, but nighthawks also roost in trees or on other elevated perches. Both lay eggs on bare ground.

Did you Know? Both species are members of the nightjar or goatsucker family. The term "goatsucker" originates from an old legend that unfairly accuses this family of drinking the milk of goats at night.

Date and Location Seen: _____

Description: 4.75". Tiny aerial bird with rapid wingbeats; often likened to a "cigar with wings". **Dusky**, with **paler grayish throat, breast**, and **rump**. Has **short, squared tail**.

Similar Species: Larger White-throated Swift (p. 199) has more contrasting black and white plumage. Swallows have looser flight on more flexed wings, usually have contrastingly pale underparts.

Voice: High rapid chippering, accelerating to insect-like trill. Very vocal around roost sites.

Where to Find: Fairly common migrant (April-May, August-September), uncommon summer resident of mature coniferous forests.

Behavior: Forages for flying insects above the canopy in coniferous forests and along waterways. Nests communally. Nest is a half circle of small twigs glued together with the birds' sticky saliva, placed on inside wall of hollow trees, or less commonly in chimneys. Large numbers roost together at night in hollow trees or in chimneys during migration.

Did you Know? Best known for their rapid and agile flight, Vaux's Swifts seldom perch unless roosting or nesting, and probably even mate on the wing. Their feet and tails are specialized for clinging to vertical surfaces.

Date and Location Seen: _____

_____

Description: 6.5″. **Blackish-brown** with **white throat** coming to a point on the lower breast. Has **white flanks and rump-sides; long tail** has shallow fork, but **usually appears pointed**. White markings are often difficult to see, but distinctive shape (long, thin wings, elongated rear body and tail) helps to identify it.

Similar Species: Adult Black Swifts (rare) have no white markings. Violet-green Swallows (p. 265) have different wing and body shapes, and different flight.

Voice: Call is long, descending series of rapid *jee-jee-jee* notes.

Where to Find: Common migrant and summer resident (April-September) of rocky cliffs and canyons. Regular along Succor Creek near Adrian, Oregon; Swan Falls near Boise, Idaho; and Wallula Gap, Washington.

Behavior: Nests colonially in cliff face crevices, often with Violet-Green Swallows. Forages high over open country for winged insects. Large flocks typically gather in the fall prior to departure.

Did you Know? The White-throated Swift mating ritual is spectacular. While high in the air, a pair will cling together facing each other with wings pointed in four directions. Then they pinwheel downward in a free fall while copulating, only separating before striking the ground.

Date and Location Seen: _____

_____

Black-chinned
Hummingbird Male

Black-chinned
Hummingbird Female

Anna's Hummingbird
Male

Anna's Hummingbird
Female

Description: 3.75"/4". BLACK-CHINNED: **Male has black chin, violet throa**t (usually appears black), **long bill, white spot behind eye; broad white collar** below throat; flanks olive; upperparts deep green; tail blackish, slightly forked. Female's chin and throat whitish, slight buff on flanks, tail with white corners. ANNA'S: **Male has brilliant rose-red crown, chin, and throat**; pale area around eye; upperparts iridescent green; underparts mostly olive-gray. Female has **variable red patch in center of throat**; underparts **grayish with greenish flanks**; tail corners white.

Similar Species: Female Anna's differentiated from female Calliope (p. 203), Broad-tailed, and Rufous (p. 205) by red throat patch and grayish breast with green flanks.

Voice: BLACK-CHINNED: Call is soft *tiup*. ANNA'S: Call is sharp, high *stit*.

Where to Find: BLACK-CHINNED: Fairly common summer resident (April-September) of low valleys, especially riparian areas. ANNA'S: Rare summer resident along east slope of the Cascades. Rare in residential areas throughout our region, mainly in fall and winter.

Behavior: Both species forage for flower nectar and insects in valleys. BLACK-CHINNED: Nests in riparian areas. ANNA'S: A species of residential areas. Both readily visit feeders and flower gardens.

Did you Know? Males of each species make a spectacular aerial and vocal display for females during the breeding season.

Date and Location Seen: _____

_____

Male

Female

Description: 3.25". Our smallest hummingbird; **short-billed** and **short-tailed**. MALE: **Tiny**; greenish above, pale below, with greenish flanks and **rose-red rays on the throat**. FEMALE: Like male except has buff-tinted sides, finely-spotted white throat, and **wingtips that extend beyond the tail**.

Similar Species: Very small size and short tail differentiate this species from Broad-tailed and Rufous Hummingbirds (p. 205).

Voice: Produces quiet, very high chip notes.

Where to Find: Common summer resident (April-September) in open forests, forest edges, shrub fields, and riparian areas.

Behavior: Feeds on flower nectar and tiny insects, also visits feeders. Perches and forages closer to the ground than other hummingbird species. Often nests on or near conifer tree cones where nest is well camouflaged. Also nests in riparian thickets.

Did you Know? The Calliope Hummingbird is the smallest breeding bird in North America.

Date and Location Seen: _____

_____

Broad-tailed
Hummingbird Male

Rufous Hummingbird
Male

Rufous Hummingbird
Female

Description: 3.75"/4". RUFOUS: Bill straight, dark. Male's **back, tail**, **underparts rusty-orange**; back may have variable amounts of green. Crown green, upper breast white; throat iridescent orange-red. Female's upperparts and crown green; **tail base, undertail, flanks rufous**; outer tail feathers white-tipped. Red feathering on throat varies from none up to small spot. Immature resembles female. BROAD-TAILED: Long-bodied, with **long, broad tail**. Upperparts entirely shiny green, wings dark; head has **pale white eye-ring** and eye-line; breast is white. Male has **rose-red throat**, flanks green and buff. Female's throat is finely-spotted green on white, flanks buffy. Immature resembles female.

Similar Species: Female Anna's Hummingbird (p. 201) shows no rufous coloration. Much smaller female Calliope Hummingbird (p. 203) has shorter tail.

Voice: Both species give *chip* calls. Flight feathers of male Broadtail produce diagnostic a trill.

Where to Find: BROAD-TAILED: Uncommon to rare summer resident (May-August) of high-elevation meadows and valleys of southern Idaho, southeastern and northeastern Oregon, and southwestern Montana. RUFOUS: Common migrant (April-June, August-September) and uncommon summer resident of coniferous forests.

Behavior: Both feed on flower nectar, tree sap, very small insects, and readily accept sugar water at feeders.

Did you Know? Male Rufous and Broad-tailed Hummingbirds have distinctive diving courtship displays.

Date and Location Seen: _____

_____

Male

Female

Description: 13". Distinctive, boldly plumaged waterbird with a **bushy crown** creating a large-headed appearance. Has a long, dark bill. MALE: **Blue-gray above, white below**, with a blue-gray band across the upper breast; white patch on the wings is visible in flight. FEMALE: Similar to male, but with **rusty band across the lower breast**, sides and flanks.

Similar Species: Other plunge-diving waterbirds, such as terns have very different shape and plumage.

Voice: Loud, staccato rattle usually announces the kingfisher's presence.

Where to Find: Fairly common summer resident of wetlands, streams, ponds, and lakes. Uncommon and local in winter in low-elevation areas where water remains open.

Behavior: Perches on branches of waterside trees, shrubs, or utility wires. Flies with quick, irregular rowing wingbeats. Hovers over water when foraging, then plunges to catch fish or other aquatic vertebrates and invertebrates. Aggressively defends territories. Nests in long burrows excavated in vertical earthen stream banks.

Did you Know? Like raptors, Belted Kingfishers regurgitate undigested fish bones and scales as pellets.

Date and Location Seen: _____

_____

Adult

Description: 10.75". Large, dark woodpecker of open forests. ADULT: **Upperparts are all black** with a greenish gloss. Has broad, **pale-gray collar and breast. Dark red face** is framed in black. **Underparts are pinkish**. Distinctive **rowing wing-beats** are crow-like. JUVENILE: Similar to adult, but lacks gray collar and red face.

Similar Species: Black-backed Woodpecker (p. 219) lacks red face, pale collar, and pinkish underparts.

Voice: Calls include variety of high-pitched, squeaky notes. Song is series of harsh *chur* notes.

Where to Find: Fairly common to rare migrant and summer resident (April-September), mainly in cottonwood riparian woodlands, ponderosa pine forests, and oak woodlands. Locally common in winter in oak woodlands. Regular in Tygh Valley, Oregon; Lyle and Yakima, Washington; Boise, Idaho; and National Bison Range, Montana.

Behavior: Lewis's Woodpecker has steady, buoyant flight with slow wing-beats and long glides. Mainly forages for winged insects by flycatching. Also stores fruit, berries, and acorns in tree crevices and holes for later use. Drills nest cavities in decayed trees. Most populations are migratory.

Did you Know? Lewis's Woodpecker populations are declining throughout their range because of competition from European Starlings for nest sites and habitat loss caused by human activities.

Date and Location Seen: _____

_____

Male

Female

Description: 9". Our largest and most distinctive sapsucker. MALE: **Upperparts all-black** with broad, white wing patch, white facial stripes. **Throat is red, breast is black, belly is yellow**, undertail is white. FEMALE: **Head is brown; upperparts finely barred** light and dark brown. **Breast is black**, belly is yellow, flanks and undertail are barred. Both sexes show white rump in flight.

Similar Species: Larger Northern Flicker (p. 221) similar to female Williamson's, but has boldly spotted underparts.

Voice: Call is strong *quee-ah*.

Where to Find: Fairly common to rare migrant and summer resident (March-October). Nests in mid- to high-elevation mature, open coniferous and mixed forests, especially those with western larch. Rare in winter. May be seen in central and northeastern mountains of Oregon; Okanogan Valley and Blue Mountains, Washington; Bear Basin, near McCall, Idaho; and Red Rock Lakes N.W.R., Montana.

Behavior: Omnivorous, forages for conifer sap, insects, fruit. Excavates distinctive horizontal rows of small holes in tree trunks and limbs, returning to eat sap collected in wells and insects trapped in sap. Typically hollows nest cavity in live western larch or aspen with heart rot. Male excavates new nest cavity each year.

Did you Know? Williamson's Sapsucker is the only North American woodpecker showing such striking plumage differences between the sexes. Until 1873, they were thought to be two different species.

Date and Location Seen: _____

_____

Red-naped Sapsucker

Red-breasted Sapsucker

Description: 8.5". Mottled black and white woodpeckers that have a **pale yellow belly** and a long white wing patch. RED-NAPED: Male has a **red crown and throat**, black and white-striped face, **black breast band**, and red nape spot. Female is nearly identical, usually with less red on head and throat; may have a white chin, red nape. RED-BREASTED: Has **entirely red head and breast** with white mark at the base of the bill.

Similar Species: Male Williamson's Sapsucker (p. 211) lacks red on the head, has an all-black back.

Voice: Call of both is mewing *meeah*. Territorial males "drum" in a unique rhythm, often about five rapid taps followed by gradually slowing taps.

Where to Find: RED-NAPED: Common migrant and summer resident (March-October) of coniferous forests and aspen groves. RED-BREASTED: Uncommon summer resident of east slopes of Cascades; common in Klamath and Lake Counties, Oregon; rare elsewhere. Both are rare in winter.

Behavior: Both species forage mainly for sap and insects. Drill distinctive horizontal rows of small holes in tree trunks and limbs, returning to eat sap collected in wells and insects trapped in sap. Excavate nest cavities mainly in live aspens, cottonwoods, birches, and sometimes in conifers.

Did you Know? Where the ranges of these two species overlap they often interbreed, creating various combinations of plumages.

Date and Location Seen: _____

_____

Downy Woodpecker
Male

Downy Woodpecker
Female

Hairy Woodpecker
Male

Hairy Woodpecker
Female

Description: 6.75″/9″. DOWNY: Our **smallest woodpecker**, with a black and white-patterned head, **long white back stripe**, white underparts, and white-spotted black wings. **Bill is very short**. Male has red bar on the nape, that female lacks. HAIRY: A larger version of the Downy, with relatively longer and sturdy bill.

Similar Species: American Three-toed Woodpecker (p. 219) has heavy dark barring on sides, with black-barring on a white back stripe.

Voice: DOWNY: Call is gentle *pik*. HAIRY: Gives a sharper, stronger *peek*. Both also have diagnostic rattle calls.

Where to Find: DOWNY: Uncommon, widespread resident of riparian woodlands and mixed forests, often in residential areas. HAIRY: Uncommon, shy, widespread resident of mainly coniferous forests. Makes fall altitudinal migrations to lower elevation valleys, including residential areas with large trees.

Behavior: Both feed on insects, fruit, and seeds. DOWNY: Forages on smaller trees than Hairy, often acrobatically on outer branches and twigs. HAIRY: Forages on the trunk and larger limbs of large trees; attracted to burned forests, diseased and dying trees.

Did you Know? Hairy Woodpecker has a huge range, from Alaska and Canada south to Panama. Like many such widespread birds it shows great geographical variation in size and plumage.

Date and Location Seen: _____

_____

Male

Female

Description: 9.25". **Black woodpecker with white head and throat, white wing patch.** Male has red nape that the female lacks.

Similar Species: The only North American woodpecker with a black body and white head.

Voice: Call is sharp *pitik*; "rattle" call is a loud and extended *peekikikikik*.

Where to Find: Uncommon and decreasing resident mainly in mature, open ponderosa pine and fir forests in Oregon, Washington, and Idaho. Most regular in Camp Sherman and Sisters, Oregon; Idaho City, Idaho; and south central Washington.

Behavior: Nests in snags or diseased live trees, often within ten feet of the ground. Diet is mostly insects and pine seeds.

Did you Know? Perhaps the best method for finding White-headed Woodpeckers is to first learn their unique "rattle" call, and then survey likely areas for them on foot in spring and early summer.

Date and Location Seen: _____

_____

American Three-toed Woodpecker Male

American Three-toed Woodpecker Female

Black-backed Woodpecker Male

Black-backed Woodpecker Female

Description: 8.75"/9.5". Stocky, medium-size woodpeckers with white underparts, prominent white moustache marks, and **heavily barred flanks**. Males have **yellow foreheads**. THREE-TOED: Has **variable white barring on back**. BLACK-BACKED: Has **all-black upperparts**.

Similar Species: Downy and Hairy Woodpeckers (p. 215) have white backs and lack heavily barred flanks.

Voice: THREE-TOED: Call is flat *pik*. BLACK-BACKED: Call is deep *chek* or *chuk*. Both species make rattle calls, but are often quiet and inconspicuous.

Where to Find: THREE-TOED: Uncommon and local resident of high-elevation coniferous forests. BLACK-BACKED: Uncommon resident of mid- to high-elevation coniferous forests.

Behavior: Both mostly forage for wood-boring beetle larvae and other insects by flaking conifer tree bark, but may also excavate wood for larvae. Frequently excavate low nest cavities in recently burned trees.

Did you Know? Both species are attracted to large patches of recently burned or insect-infested high-elevation conifers, where they often occur together. Look and listen for them in the spring or very early summer.

Date and Location Seen: _____

_____

Male

Female

Description: 12.5". **Large, familiar woodpecker**. Generally **light brown above** with thin, black crossbars and a **white rump**; buffy white with **round**, prominent **black spots below**. Has **black crescent across the chest**. In flight, our "Red-shafted" birds show **reddish color in wings and tail**. Male's red "whisker" mark is absent in female.

Similar Species: Unmistakable, but see female Williamson's Sapsucker (p. 211); the sapsucker has shorter bill, yellow body, and lacks color in the wings.

Voice: Call is piercing *keeeew*; also gives muffled *wur-wur-wur* in flight and a *wick-a-wick-a* series. Territorial birds give a long *wik-wik-wik-wik* series, often followed by drumming.

Where to Find: Common resident and migrant (March-April, September-October).

Behavior: Usually forages on tree trunks and limbs, but also feeds on ants on the ground. Flashy wing color shows prominently in undulating flight. In spring, males often hammer on metallic and wooden objects (often buildings) to create sounding boards for territorial defense.

Did you Know? Eastern/boreal "Yellow-shafted" and western "Red-shafted" flickers hybridize extensively where their ranges overlap. "Yellow-shafted" flickers along with those showing intermediate or combined characters are occasionally seen in our region.

Date and Location Seen: _____

_____

Description: 16.5". Our largest (**crow-size**) woodpecker that is long-necked, broad-winged, and long-tailed. **All-black**, with a **bright red crest**, and **black and white striped face and neck**; has white underwings and small white patches on upperwings; large chisel-like dark bill. MALE: Has **red crown, forecrown**, and **mustache mark**. FEMALE: Same as male, but with **dark forecrown** and **black mustache mark**.

Similar Species: Much larger than all other woodpeckers, pattern is distinctive.

Voice: Call is series of loud, deep *kuk* notes.

Where to Find: Uncommon resident of mature coniferous and deciduous forests. Frequently seen at Ponderosa State Park in McCall, Idaho; Glacier N.P., Montana; and the Blue Mountains of Oregon and Washington.

Behavior: Diet is mostly wood-boring insects. Obtains much of its food from well-decayed snags. Creates diagnostic large rectangular holes in snags. Nests in large coniferous and deciduous trees, and excavates new nest each year. Occasionally makes altitudinal movements in the fall and winter.

Did you Know? Despite their huge size and raucous, loud calls, Pileated Woodpeckers are shy and often fly away or move to the backside of a tree when humans approach them.

Date and Location Seen: _____

_____

Western Wood Pewee

Olive-sided Flycatcher

Description: 6.25"/7.5". WOOD-PEWEE: Drab, peak-headed flycatcher with **dark olive-gray upperparts, dull olive-gray breast**, paler gray throat and undertail. **Wings are long and pointed**, tail is moderately long. Indistinct grayish wing-bars; **no eye-ring**. OLIVE-SIDED: Large, **big-headed** flycatcher with faintly streaked **olive sides** and **white stripe down the center of the underparts**. Dark olive-gray above; white tufts may show above wings when perched. Wings long and pointed, tail moderately short.

Similar Species: Willow Flycatcher (p. 227) has smaller head, shorter wings, and flicks its tail.

Voice: WOOD-PEWEE: Call is burry descending *pee-urrrr*; song is similar to call. OLIVE-SIDED: Call is *pip-pip-pip*; song is loud *pip-WEE-deer* ("Quick, three beers!").

Where to Find: WOOD-PEWEE: Common migrant and summer resident (May-September) in open, dry coniferous forests and riparian woodlands. OLIVE-SIDED: Uncommon migrant and summer resident (May-September) of coniferous forest edges and clearings. Rare in migration elsewhere.

Behavior: Both species make sallies from exposed tree perches (Wood-pewee sits in mid-canopy, Olive-sided occupies tall tree tops) to capture flying insects, and often return to their original perch.

Did you Know? Olive-sided Flycatchers favor burned forests, because burns provide open foraging areas, snag perches, and abundant flying insects.

Date and Location Seen: _____

_____

Willow Flycatcher
Spring

Pacific-Slope/Cordilleran
Flycatcher

Description: 5.75"/5.5". WILLOW: **Upperparts are tinged gold-en-olive** with dull whitish wing-bars and whitish underparts. **Lacks eye-ring** and has a relatively long, **broad bill. Throat is whitish. Larger and longer-tailed than most other** *Empidonax* flycatchers. PACIFIC-SLOPE/CORDILLERAN: Virtually identical species. **Yellowish underparts (including throat)** and yellow-tinged olive upperparts are usually distinctive, but the dullest birds may be distinguished by **teardrop-shaped eye-ring** (pointed at rear), peaked crown, orangish lower bill and hint of pale yellow on the throat.

Similar Species: Dusky (p. 231) and Hammond's (p. 229) Flycatchers have a distinct eye-ring and lack the yellowish throat.

Voice: WILLOW: Call is sharp *whit*; song is burry *witz-beeer* or *fitz bew*. PACIFIC-SLOPE/CORDILLERAN: Call is up-slurred *psee-eeet* or *pseeeet*.

Where to Find: WILLOW: Common migrant and summer resident (May-September) of riparian wetlands and willow thickets. PACIFIC-SLOPE/CORDILLERAN: Uncommon migrant and summer resident (April-September) of coniferous forests, aspens, and riparian woodlands.

Behavior: WILLOW: Forages for insects and nests in willow thickets. PACIFIC-SLOPE/CORDILLERAN: Both catch insects in the air and glean foliage of trees and shrubs. Heard more often than seen. Nest in trees, on ledges, in outbuildings, and under bridges.

Did you Know? Cordilleran and Pacific-slope Flycatchers can only be differentiated by voice and geographic range.

Date and Location Seen: _____

_____

Description: 5.5". Small Empidonax flycatcher, with a **tiny, mostly dark and narrow bill**, relatively short tail, **olive-gray breast, grayish head**, and long wingtips. White eye-ring is broadest at the rear. The large head, tiny bill, and eye-ring give this small flycatcher a kinglet-like appearance.

Similar Species: Slimmer Dusky Flycatcher (p. 231) has longer tail, shorter wings. Slightly smaller Least Flycatcher (rare) has a wider, paler bill, more prominent eye-ring, and creamy-white breast.

Voice: Call is high, soft *peep*; song is three-part phrase *si-pik swi-vrk gra-vik*.

Where to Find: Common migrant and summer resident (April-September) of mature coniferous forests with closed canopy; less common in open forests and aspens. More widespread in migration.

Behavior: Lifts tail forcefully upward, also flicks wings. Forages within canopy of shady forests, making quick sallies for insects. Migrants often use more open habitats.

Did you Know? Unlike the closely-related Dusky Flycatcher, Hammond's undergoes its complete annual molt before it leaves its breeding grounds, and therefore migrates south later in autumn.

Date and Location Seen: _____

_____

Dusky Flycatcher

Gray Flycatcher

Description: 5.75"/6". Small, slender flycatchers with gray-ish upperparts, **whitish or yellowish underparts, prominent whitish eye-rings**, dark gray wings with **prominent pale wing-bars**, and **long tails**. DUSKY: Has narrow, **dark bill**. GRAY: Narrow, **pale bill with a dark tip**.

Similar Species: Hammond's Flycatcher (p. 229) is more compact with a shorter tail and very small, narrow bill.

Voice: Both species give dry *whit* calls. DUSKY: Song has three phrases, a high, fast *sibit*, a rough, nasal *tuwerp*, and clear, high *sweet*; notes may be sung in any order. GRAY: Song is rough *chu-lup chu-lup*.

Where to Find: Both are common migrants and summer residents (April-September). DUSKY: Occurs in dry, open coniferous, aspen, and juniper forests with shrubby understories. GRAY: Nests in dry woodlands and shrublands, mainly in sagebrush and junipers. Also occurs in open ponderosa pine habitats with shrubs.

Behavior: DUSKY: Forages for insects on or around trees and shrubs. Typically flies out from perches to catch insects on the wing. GRAY: Usually perches low and gleans insects above and around shrubs, often dropping down to the ground.

Did you Know? Dusky and Gray Flycatchers may be distinguished by their individual tail-wagging habits. Dusky flicks its tail upward and then down, whereas Gray wags its tail gently down and then up.

Date and Location Seen: _____

_____

Description: 7.5". Open-country flycatcher that is **grayish above** with a **salmon-colored belly** and a **contrastingly blackish tail**. Juveniles have cinnamon wing-bars.

Similar Species: Distinctive.

Voice: Call is rich, down-slurred whistle *pdeeer*. Song alternates between downslurred *pdeeew* and rising *pidireep*.

Where to Find: Common migrant and summer resident (February-September) of dry open country, uncommon in winter along the Snake River Canyon in southwestern Idaho. Rare elsewhere in winter.

Behavior: Perches openly on fences, buildings, plant stems, boulders, and bare ground. Most foraging takes place at ground level. Often dips and spreads tail in a broad, shallow arc when perched. Nests wherever there is a sheltered ledge or cavity, usually on cliff faces, in trees, under rocks, or on building ledges. Among the first migrants to arrive in spring, often when snow is still present.

Did you Know? Say's Phoebes have a huge latitudinal breeding range from the Arctic Ocean shore in western Alaska south to central Mexico.

Date and Location Seen: _____

_____

Description: 8.5". Medium-size, slender flycatcher with a long tail and bushy crown. **Upperparts** are **grayish-brown**; throat is whitish; **breast is pale gray; belly and undertail** are **pale yellow; wings** are **dark grayish brown with whitish wing-bars and rust-edged flight feathers**. Tail is grayish-brown edged with rust.

Similar Species: Western Kingbird (p. 237) is similar but lacks rusty edges on wings and tail, has bright yellow belly.

Voice: Call is loud *prrt* or *prip-wheer*; song is *ka-BRICK*.

Where to Find: Uncommon to rare and local migrant and summer resident (May-September) of open juniper or mixed oak/ponderosa pine forests. Range is central and southern Oregon, south-central Washington, and southern edge of Idaho. Rare elsewhere.

Behavior: Builds nest in natural cavities or nest boxes. Diet is mainly insects gleaned from foliage or ground, also small berries. Occasionally feeds on small vertebrates. Often vocally and physically aggressive toward other birds when defending its territory.

Did you Know? Ash-throated Flycatchers obtain moisture from the food they eat, an important adaptation for life in arid country.

Date and Location Seen: _____

_____

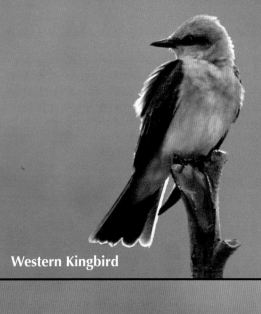

Western Kingbird

Eastern Kingbird

Description: 8.75"/8.5". WESTERN: Has **yellow belly. Pale gray upperparts**, head and breast; white throat provides little contrast. **Black tail has thin, white border along sides**. EASTERN: Dark gray above (darkest on head), **white below**, with **white tail tip**.

Similar Species: Ash-throated Flycatcher (p. 235) has rusty edges to wing and tail feathers, paler overall.

Voice: WESTERN: Calls include sharp bik and various sputtering notes; song is *pik pik peek PEEK-a-loo* crescendo. EASTERN: Call is buzzy *kzeer*; song is series of sharp, sputtering notes.

Where to Find: WESTERN: Common migrant and summer resident (April-September) in dry, open rangeland, agricultural areas, and open woodlands throughout the region. EASTERN: Common migrant and summer resident (May-September) in open areas and riparian woodlands, usually near water.

Behavior: Both species sally from high perches to catch insects; Westerns typically from utility poles or open grown shade trees and Easterns from streamside cottonwoods or willows. They also eat fruit. Both species build nests in trees, but Westerns also frequently nest on utility poles.

Did you Know? Both kingbirds are fearlessly aggressive in their defense of their nests, and will vociferously drive off or physically attack much larger birds that haplessly fly by.

Date and Location Seen: _____

_____

Loggerhead
Shrike

Northern Shrike

LOGGERHEAD SHRIKE/NORTHERN SHRIKE
Lanius ludovicianus / Lanius excubitor

Description: 9"/10". Sleek, bull-headed, long-tailed predatory songbirds with **bold black masks**; underparts pale; black wings and tails have white patches. Thick **black bill is hooked at the tip**. LOGGERHEAD: Adult has medium gray head and back, broad **mask crosses over base of lower bill. Bill is short and stubby**. NORTHERN: Adult has pearl-gray head and back; **black mask does not cross over base of lower bill**. Juvenile like adult, with **rusty wash and distinct scaling on underparts**, faded plumage and paler bill, faint white eye-ring.

Similar Species: Northern Mockingbird (rare) lacks black mask, has narrow, pointed bill.

Voice: LOGGERHEAD: Call is harsh *jaa*. NORTHERN: Call is nasal *fay fay*.

Where to Find: LOGGERHEAD: Uncommon and local migrant and summer resident (February-September) of open shrublands, rare in winter. NORTHERN: Uncommon migrant and winter resident (September-April) in open areas. Abundance varies from year to year.

Behavior: Both perch openly on fence lines, tops of shrubs, pouncing on prey (large insects, small vertebrates) with short flights. Flight is rapid and direct, often ending in a quick climb to perch.

Did you Know? Unlike raptors, shrikes lack powerful feet for grasping and dismembering prey, so they often impale prey on thorns or barbed wire to facilitate feeding or to store for later use. This has earned them the nickname "butcher bird".

Date and Location Seen: _____

_____

239

Cassin's Vireo

Plumbeous Vireo

Description: 5.5"/5.75". Stocky, short-tailed vireos that have heavy bills, whitish underparts, **bold white "spectacles"**, and **whitish wing-bars**. CASSIN'S: Upperparts are **olive-gray**; has **pale yellow flanks** and gray head. PLUMBEOUS: **Upperparts are all slate-gray**, with **grayish or pale yellowish flanks**.

Similar Species: Red-eyed Vireo (p. 243) has a long, flat crown and a bold white eyebrow. Blue-headed Vireo (very rare) has blue-gray crown and face that are sharply demarked from pure white throat and greenish back; also has bolder white wing-bars and more distinctive yellow flanks. Warbling Vireo (p. 243) lacks white wing-bars and "spectacles".

Voice: Both give rapid, harsh scolding calls and similar burry, whistled songs with notes inflected upward and downward. Cassin's song has higher-pitched notes.

Where to Find: CASSIN'S: Fairly common migrant and summer resident (April-September) of dry, open coniferous or mixed forests. PLUMBEOUS: Uncommon to rare and local resident of riparian woodlands in southern Idaho and southeastern Oregon. Often seen along Mink Creek, near Pocatello, Idaho.

Behavior: Both glean insects slowly and deliberately in upper tree canopy; also hover-glean and flycatch. Persistent singers, often heard throughout the day during the breeding season.

Did you Know? These two species were formerly conspecific with the eastern-dwelling Blue-headed Vireo and were known as Solitary Vireos.

Date and Location Seen: _____

_____

Warbling Vireo

Red-eyed Vireo

Description: 5.5"/6". These vireos **lack wing-bars**. WARBLING: **Plain brownish-olive above**, whitish below, with **distinct pale eyebrow**. RED-EYED: Has **uniform olive-green upperparts**, white and pale yellow below. **Long, flat gray crown** sharply borders **conspicuous white eyebrow; dark eye-line** runs through **red eye**; has long, heavy bill.

Similar Species: Cassin's Vireo (p. 241) has white "spectacles" and wing-bars.

Voice: WARBLING: Call is harsh, nasal *meeerish*; song is rapid warble of high and low notes. RED-EYED: Calls include soft, nasal *meerf* or descending *myaah*; song is a continuous, hurried series of whistled notes.

Where to Find: WARBLING: Common migrant and summer resident (April-September) of riparian areas and young shrubby forests. RED-EYED: Uncommon migrant, rare and local to fairly common summer resident (May-September) of deciduous riparian woodlands, especially cottonwoods. Found in Blue and Wallowa Mountains of Oregon, mountains of northeastern Washington, and Rocky Mountains of Idaho and Montana.

Behavior: Both glean for insects slowly and deliberately in upper tree canopy. Persistent singers, they can often be heard throughout the day even on the hottest days when other songbirds are silent.

Did you Know? Timber harvest and fire open up coniferous forest canopies, creating shrubby habitats that favor Warbling Vireos.

Date and Location Seen: _____

Description: 11.5″. ADULT: Has **dark gray upperparts, light gray underparts**, and **dark crown; face, neck, and forehead are white**. Bill is dark, short, and stout. IMMATURE: Dark sooty gray with whitish moustachial stripe.

Similar Species: Clark's Nutcracker (p. 253) has black wings with prominent white patches, a mostly white tail, and long bill.

Voice: Call is short series of soft, whistled notes, commonly a clear *wheeoo*.

Where to Find: Uncommon resident of mid- to high-elevation boreal and subalpine coniferous forests.

Behavior: Mainly forages from perches, flying from tree to tree in search of various foods, including insects, fruit, small vertebrates, and carrion. Gregarious, often traveling through the forest in family groups. Sometimes makes altitudinal migrations to lower elevation areas in late fall and winter.

Did you Know? Gray Jays are bold and inquisitive, and quickly learn to accept food from human hands.

Date and Location Seen: _____

_____

Steller's Jay

Blue Jay

Description: 11.5"/11". STELLER'S: **Blackish crested head** shows white eye crescents, forehead marks, and streaks on throat. Back is charcoal gray; all **other plumage cobalt blue**. Wings and tail show fine black barring. BLUE: **All-pale blue upperparts and grayish-white underparts**. Has white wing markings and tail corners, fine black bands on wings and tail. **Head has distinctive blue crest; pale throat** outlined by **black "necklace"**.

Similar Species: Western Scrub-Jay (p. 249) lacks crest, has faint blue breast band.

Voice: STELLER'S: Call is harsh *shek shek shek*. BLUE: Common call is *jaaaay*.

Where to Find: STELLER'S: Common resident of coniferous and mixed forests. Frequents lowland residential areas in winter. BLUE: Uncommon or rare and local resident of deciduous or mixed park-like forests, often residential areas, in western Montana valleys. Rare and irregular fall migrant and winter resident (October-February) elsewhere. Range is expanding in the region.

Behavior: Both omnivorous. Forage for seeds, fruits, insects and other invertebrates; also feed on small vertebrates, other birds' eggs and nestlings. Steller's commonly moves downslope in fall to low-elevation valleys in search of food; mixed feeding flocks of these two species readily visit bird feeders. Both are very vocal outside of the breeding season, quiet and secretive around breeding territories.

Did you Know? Jays are judged to be among the most intelligent of birds.

Date and Location Seen: _____

Description: 11.5". A slender and long-tailed jay. **Deep blue above** with a **brown back patch**, pale gray underparts separated from the white throat by a **partial blue breast band**. JUVENILE: Like adult, but mostly gray-brown on the head; has indistinct gray collar.

Similar Species: Pinyon Jay (p. 251) is entirely blue, lacks pale underparts. Steller's Jay (p. 247) has cobalt blue plumage with a blackish crested head.

Voice: Main calls are harsh upslurred *jaaay* or *jreee* and (usually in flight) a rapid series of *sheelp, sheelp* notes.

Where to Find: Common resident of deciduous and juniper woodlands from Klickitat County, Washington south through central Oregon, eastward to the Warner Mountains, and locally in southern Idaho. Rare elsewhere.

Behavior: Bold and familiar, easily tamed in backyards with peanuts or sunflower seeds. Versatile omnivores that eat acorns, seeds, insects, and fruits; often songbird eggs and nestlings. Nests are usually well concealed in trees or shrubs. Like other jays, usually very secretive near their nest sites.

Did you Know? Western Scrub-Jay is expanding its range eastward in Oregon and Washington, and sightings well away from their established range are increasing.

Date and Location Seen: _____

_____

Description: 10.5". Medium-size jay, **all dusty-blue** (except for whitish streaks on throat) with long, tapered dark bill, and relatively short tail. Immature is dull bluish-gray.

Similar Species: Western Scrub-Jay (p. 249) has gray back and light gray underparts.

Voice: Call is nasal cawing *qwee qwee qwee*.

Where to Find: Fairly common, but local resident of foothills and low-elevation mountain slopes where pinyon and juniper forests occur in central Oregon, southeastern Idaho, and south central Montana. Wanders widely to surrounding areas after breeding. Good locations include the Sisters and Cabin Lake Guard Station areas, Oregon and near Stone, Idaho.

Behavior: Large flocks often wander long distances in search of available pine seed crops. In times of pine seed shortage, diet can also include acorns, juniper berries, cultivated grains, and even reptiles or other small vertebrates. Nests colonially, and forms complex social organizations. Flock remains together throughout the year.

Did you Know? Although omnivorous, Pinyon Jays have evolved to become pine seed feeding specialists.

Date and Location Seen: _____

_____

Description: 12″. Large and **gray** overall with a **white patch on black wings**; has broad white borders to a short, black tail. Undertail is white. Has a long, pointed black bill.

Similar Species: Gray Jay (p. 245) lacks black wings and tail, has shorter bill.

Voice: A long harsh *kraaaaaaaa*.

Where to Find: Fairly common resident of coniferous forests. Wanders widely in years when pine seed crops are poor. Common and conspicuous at Crater Lake National Park, Oregon; Glacier National Park, Montana, and other areas of alpine and sub-alpine forests.

Behavior: Mainly feeds on pine seeds. Begins nesting in late winter, relying on pine seed caches for food supply. After young are fledged in spring, moves upslope to sub-alpine zones until fall. At times, wanders extensively in search of food, sometimes in large flocks.

Did you Know? Clark's Nutcracker has an incredible memory, enabling it to find most of the thousands of seeds during winter that it cached in the fall.

Date and Location Seen: _____

_____

Description: 19". Fairly large corvid with **black head, upperparts**, and undertail area. **White flanks, shoulder patch, and belly**; and **iridescent green wings and tail. Tail is long and wedge-shaped**. In flight, **broad white wing patch** is prominent.

Similar Species: Differentiated from other jays and Clark's Nutcracker (p. 253) by combination of black upperparts, white belly, and long tail.

Voice: Call is rising *jeeeek* and rapid *shek shek shek*.

Where to Find: Common resident of rangelands or other open areas, especially riparian areas with scattered deciduous trees and shrubs.

Behavior: Omnivorous. Feeds mostly on insects in summer and wide variety of foods including seeds, berries, small vertebrates, and carrion in other seasons. Builds large stick nests with domed canopies in shrubs or trees, and forages in a variety of open habitats, including agricultural and residential areas. Forms large, noisy roosts in winter, sometimes numbering several hundred birds. Like other corvids, magpies are gregarious, vocal, and intelligent.

Did you Know? Many bird species use abandoned old magpie nests for their nests and roost sites, including hawks and owls.

Date and Location Seen: _____

_____

Description: 17.5", wingspan 39". Familiar large, chunky, **all-black** bird with a **heavy black bill, and square or slightly rounded tail**.

Similar Species: Common Raven (p. 259) has longer, more pointed wings, longer wedge-shaped tail, heavier bill, and shaggy throat feathers.

Voice: Call is repeated *caw caw caw*.

Where to Find: Common widespread resident of low-elevation open valleys, most often around agricultural and residential areas with trees. Concentrations occur in valleys with open water and abundant food resources in winter.

Behavior: Intelligent and inquisitive omnivores that forage in many ways, including scavenging dead animals, availing themselves of abundant seed crops or insects, preying upon small vertebrates, or gleaning through trash. Bold and abundant, they are usually wary of people. Gather into large winter flocks to feed and roost.

Did you Know? Although West Nile virus has been identified in more than 200 species of birds, American Crows have been one of the most frequent victims of the disease.

Date and Location Seen: _____

_____

Description: 24", wingspan 46". Our largest songbird, being almost half again the length and twice the weight of the American Crow. **All black**, with long pointed wings, **wedge-shaped tail, very heavy black bill**, and thin, lance-like feathers on the throat.

Similar Species: Smaller American Crow (p. 257) has square or slightly rounded tail, and much different voice.

Voice: Common calls are deep, resonant croaks. Also gives hollow knocking calls and higher gurgling notes.

Where to Find: Common widespread resident of open rangelands, foothills, and mountains. Visits agricultural and residential areas, especially after the breeding season.

Behavior: Unlike crows, ravens routinely soar high in the air like hawks. Omnivorous, it often feeds on road kills along highways, refuse at landfills and dumpsters. An effective predator, it also takes rodents, reptiles, and eggs and young of many bird species. Builds a large stick nest, usually on cliff faces or in trees.

Did you Know? Bold and resourceful, ravens are considered among the most intelligent of all birds.

Date and Location Seen: _____

_____

Male

Juvenile

Description: 7.25". Flocking sparrow-like bird of open country. Pinkish-brown above, mostly white below. **Tail is black with brown center and white edges**. MALE: Has **black bib** on breast, black cheek patch, black bar across forecrown with small projecting feathers ("horns"). **Throat and eyebrow yellow or white**. FEMALE: Duller with less contrasting pattern. JUVENILE: Streaky, suggesting a sparrow or pipit.

Similar Species: American Pipit (p. 321) is darker, more slender, and streaked on breast. Snow Bunting and Lapland Longspur (p. 377) have much more patterned upperparts and heads.

Voice: Flight calls include *tseep, tew*, and *zip* notes. Song starts with *terp* notes, followed by rising, tinkling flourish; often given in sustained flight.

Where to Find: Common migrant; summer and winter resident in sparsely vegetated, open areas.

Behavior: A ground bird, but will perch on low shrubs and fence lines. Found in pairs in the breeding season, but in fall and winter gathers into large flocks that wheel about low over open fields.

Did you Know? Horned Larks perform elaborate breeding displays. A male flies up high (often hundreds of feet) into the sky, sings his high, tinkling songs above a prospective mate as he circles her ground position, then folds his wings and plunges to the ground.

Date and Location Seen: _____

_____

Male

Male

Female
First-year

Description: 5.75". Bi-colored swallow, **entirely dark above** (including through the eyes) and **white below**. **Tail is slightly forked**. MALE: Deep **iridescent steel blue** to blue-green above, pure white below. FEMALE: Variable; usually much duller above than male, with slaty-brown cast. JUVENILE: Brown above, variable tinge of gray across the breast.

Similar Species: Smaller Violet-green Swallow (p. 265) is shorter-tailed, has white around the eyes, and white patches on the sides of rump. Bank Swallow (p. 269) resembles juvenile Tree but has distinct brown breast band, pale brown rump and pale area behind cheeks. Northern Rough-winged Swallow (p. 267) resembles juvenile Tree, but has a brown throat.

Voice: Calls have rich, liquid quality: *treep or chirp*; song is series of liquid chirps and whistles.

Where to Find: Common migrant (March-May, July-October) and summer resident, often concentrated around wetlands, rivers, and lakes.

Behavior: Like all swallows, spends most of the day on the wing foraging for flying insects. Perches on wires, bare limbs, and bulrushes; usually over water. Nests in cavities in riparian trees; uses nest boxes near lakes and marshes.

Did you Know? Hardy Tree Swallows winter farther north than any other American swallows, and are the earliest to arrive in our region in spring.

Date and Location Seen: _____

_____

Male

Male

Description: 5.25″. Small, **short-tailed, green-backed** swallow with white underparts, **white on the face over the eye**, and **white sides to the rump**. MALE: Has bright felt-green back and crown, violet rump. FEMALE: Has duller back and rump; face pattern is more obscure.

Similar Species: Tree Swallow (p. 263) has white underparts, but lacks white over the eye and shows a deep bluish-green back.

Voice: Most common call is sharp *chilp* or *chip-lip*; song is rhythmic series of *chip, tseep*, and *chew* notes.

Where to Find: Common migrant (April-May, August-September) and summer resident of rocky cliffs and canyons.

Behavior: Nests colonially on cliff face crevices (often with White-throated Swifts), also in tree cavities, on buildings and other man-made structures, and in nest boxes.

Did you Know? In summer, Violet-green Swallows can be active and very vocal well before dawn.

Date and Location Seen: _____

_____

Description: 5.5″. **Dull brownish head and upperparts,** dingy white underparts with a **diffuse, pale brownish wash on throat, breast, and sides.** Tail is squared or very slightly notched; wings are long. JUVENILE: Resembles adult, but with cinnamon wing-bars.

Similar Species: Similar juvenile Tree Swallow (p. 263) has a white throat. Smaller Bank Swallow (p. 269) is shorter winged, has a paler back, and a distinct breast band contrasting with its white throat.

Voice: Call is low, coarse *prriit.*

Where to Find: Fairly common migrant and summer resident (April-September) along rivers and other bodies of water at low- to mid-elevations.

Behavior: Flight is buoyant, with swept-back wingbeats. Often forages over water but also over open fields and meadows. Nests in holes in earthen banks, but also uses artificial sites under bridges or other structures. Does not nest colonially.

Did you Know? The Rough-winged Swallow gets its name from small serrations on the outer edge of its outermost flight feathers. Interestingly, the function of these serrations remains unknown.

Date and Location Seen: _____

_____

Description: 5.25". North America's **smallest swallow**. Head and back are grayish-brown, wings and tail darker. **Underparts, including throat and cheek, are white** with **distinct brown breast band**.

Similar Species: Northern Rough-winged Swallow (p. 267) has dingy gray throat and breast, lacks distinct breast band. Juvenile Tree Swallow (p. 263) has incomplete pale gray breast band.

Voice: Call is dry, harsh *churr*, often repeated rapidly.

Where to Find: Common migrant (April-May, July-September) and locally common summer resident of open, lowland areas in valleys. The largest colonies are usually along rivers, especially the Columbia River in Washington and Snake River in Idaho.

Behavior: Forages on the wing for flying insects, usually in flocks flying over ponds, lakes, and rivers. Diagnostic flight is fast, with fluttery, shallow wingbeats. Nests colonially in erodible vertical streamside banks or gravel pit walls. Soils at nest sites are usually sandy and unstable, forcing colonies to occasionally move when banks collapse. In late summer, colonies coalesce into large homogenous flocks prior to migration.

Did you Know? Although Bank Swallows occur in widely distributed colonies during the breeding season, large flocks gather by the hundreds or even thousands at prime feeding locations in late summer just prior to migration.

Date and Location Seen: _____

_____

Description: 5.5". **Square-tailed** swallow with **chestnut throat and cheek that contrasts with white underparts. White forehead** contrasts with dark cap; upperparts with white back streaking and distinct, **deep buff rump** patch. Wings broader and relatively shorter than Tree or Barn Swallows. JUVENILE: Duller and less strongly patterned, with variable white spotting in dull brown throat.

Similar Species: Juvenile Barn Swallow (p. 273) has dark forehead, strongly forked tail.

Voice: Calls include rough *vrrrt* or *veer* notes, a more musical *veeew*, and a prolonged song of grating, creaking notes.

Where to Find: Common migrant and summer resident (April-September) in open areas. Large colonies occur on cliffs along waterways, especially in the Columbia Basin, Washington; Owyhee and Malheur Rivers in Oregon; and Snake River in Idaho.

Behavior: Often seen in large flocks. Typical flight includes circling and steep upward climbs. Builds a distinctive gourd-shaped nest from mud pellets, usually located under protective ledge or roof. The largest colonies are on cliff faces, but smaller colonies occur under bridges, on dam faces, and on barns or other human structures.

Did you Know? Gray-crowned and Black Rosy-Finches frequently roost in abandoned Cliff Swallow nests in winter.

Date and Location Seen: _____

_____

Description: 6.75". Large, slender swallow with a **very long, deeply forked tail**. MALE: Deep steel-blue above, with a **chestnut forehead and throat, orangish underparts**. White spots show on spread tail. FEMALE: Resembles male, but tail is shorter; underparts are paler. JUVENILE: Has even shorter, but still strongly forked tail; underparts are whitish-buff.

Similar Species: Shorter-tailed juveniles can suggest Cliff Swallow (p. 271), but have dark rump and prominent tail notch.

Voice: Call is scratchy *vit* or *vit-WHEET*; song combines *vit* calls with other scratchy notes.

Where to Find: Common migrant (March-April, August-October) and summer resident, uncommon at higher elevations and in urban areas.

Behavior: Forages on the wing for flying insects; usually flies low over open fields or water. Nests almost completely on human structures such as bridges, barns, and other structures with vertical or horizontal walls or beams that are under cover. Does not form dense colonies, though several pairs often nest in the same structure. Flocks of thousands gather in late summer prior to migration.

Did you Know? The Barn Swallow's various subspecies nest over nearly the entire northern hemisphere.

Date and Location Seen: _____

_____

Black-capped
Chickadee

Juniper Titmouse

Description: 5.25"/5.75. CHICKADEE: Small. **White cheek patch separates black head and throat**. Tiny, dark bill, gray back, pale gray or buff flanks, white underparts. TITMOUSE: **All-gray bird** (paler underparts) with **short crest on head** (sometimes not visible); has dark eyes, small dark bill, and relatively long tail.

Similar Species: Mountain chickadee (p. 277) has white eyebrow and gray underparts.

Voice: CHICKADEE: Call is clear *chick a dee dee dee*; song is high, whistled *fee-bee*, with second note lower than first. TITMOUSE: Call is rapid *sisisi*; song consists of repeated *jijiji jijiji jijiji* phrases.

Where to Find: CHICKADEE: Common resident of riparian woodlands, deciduous or mixed forests, and residential areas. TITMOUSE: Fairly common to rare and local resident of juniper woodlands in southern Idaho and southeastern Oregon. Seen at Massacre Rocks State Park, Idaho and near Adel, Oregon.

Behavior: Both species forage for insects by gleaning, hovering, and probing vegetation. Also feed on seeds and readily accept suet and bird seed at feeders. They nest in tree cavities, occasionally in nest boxes. Form foraging flocks outside of the breeding season, often with other species. Often mob predatory birds.

Did you Know? Chickadees are capable of going into a night torpor, which saves energy.

Date and Location Seen: _____

_____

Mountain Chickadee

Chesnut-backed Chickadee

Description: 5.25"/4.75". Small, acrobatic, and unwary birds of coniferous forests that have dark crowns and throats with **contrasting white cheek patches**, grayish wings. MOUNTAIN: Has gray upperparts, grayish-white lowerparts, **black crown and throat**, and bold **white eyebrow**. CHESTNUT-BACKED: Smaller, shorter-tailed. Has **dark brown crown and throat**, rich **chestnut back and flanks**.

Similar Species: Black-capped Chickadee (p. 275) lacks white eyebrow, chestnut back and flanks.

Voice: MOUNTAIN: Call is harsh *shika zee zee*; song is whistled *see bee bee*. CHESTNUT-BACKED: Calls include high, buzzy *zee dee* notes

Where to Find: MOUNTAIN: Common resident of montane coniferous forests. CHESTNUT-BACKED: Uncommon resident of moist coniferous forests. Both occur in riparian woodlands and residential areas in winter.

Behavior: Both species forage, often acrobatically, by gleaning insects from the surfaces of leaves and needles. They use tree cavities for nesting and excitedly mob predatory birds. Both species make irregular seasonal movements in response to available food resources, form post-breeding feeding flocks, and readily accept bird seed at bird feeders.

Did you Know? Both species cache food items, including bird seed, for later retrieval and consumption.

Date and Location Seen: _____

_____

Bushtit Male

Bushtit Female

Blue-gray Gnatcatcher
Breeding Male

Blue-gray Gnatcatcher
Non-breeding

Description: 4.5"/4". BUSHTIT: **Tiny**, gray, plump, and **long-tailed**. Crown and flanks are brownish. Bill is short, stubby, black. Eyes dark (male); creamy white (female). GNATCATCHER: **Tiny. Upperparts** bluish-gray (breeding male); **gray** (female). **Underparts white. Tail** is **long** and **black above**, with **white outer feathers**. Has bold **white eye-ring**. Flanks and undertail light gray. Female and immature paler, bill is small and thin.

Similar Species: Larger Juniper Titmouse (p. 275) is entirely gray.

Voice: BUSHTIT: Flocks give constant, rapid twittering *pit pit pit*; other short notes include *tsee* or *spik*. GNATCATCHER: Call is soft, but emphatic *spee*; song is series of soft, warbling notes.

Where to Find: BUSHTIT: Uncommon to rare and local resident of eastern Oregon, Columbia Basin of Washington, and southern Idaho. Found in open woodlands, brushy riparian areas, sagebrush-juniper habitats, and residential areas. GNATCATCHER: Uncommon and local summer resident of riparian areas and juniper forests in southern portions of Idaho and Oregon.

Behavior: BUSHTIT: Acrobatically gleans insects and spiders from small twigs. Flocks may consist of a dozen to several dozen birds that move quickly through shrubs and cross gaps in single-file. Builds distinctive gourd-shaped nest. GNATCATCHER: Feeds near tips of branches, stays constantly in motion.

Did you Know? Bushtits are found from southwestern British Columbia to Guatemala; their closest relatives live in Eurasia.

Date and Location Seen: _____

_____

Description: 4.5". Our only nuthatch with a **black line through the eye and a white eyebrow**. Crown is black (male) or gray (female), upperparts are gray, and **underparts are cinnamon** (paler in female).

Similar Species: White-breasted Nuthatch (p. 283) has white underparts and face, and a rust-colored undertail. Pygmy Nuthatch (p. 285) lacks the white eyebrow.

Voice: Call is weak, nasal *yenk yenk yenk*.

Where to Find: Common resident of coniferous forests, but numbers are highly variable; dependant upon available food supply. Uncommon and irregular migrant and winter resident of low-elevation valleys.

Behavior: Feeds on insects, spiders, conifer cone seeds, and bird seed or suet at bird feeders. Nests in cavities in snags and branches. Acrobatic, probes crevices in tree bark and climbs down tree trunks head first. Stores food for later use under bark, in holes, and in the ground.

Did you Know? Red-breasted Nuthatch is an irruptive species that will evacuate an area when the cone seed crop is low, and migrate elsewhere in search of food.

Date and Location Seen: _____

Male

Description: 5.75". Small, stubby-tailed gray and white climbing bird with a **dark crown**. Has a **white face** and underparts; **rufous area under tail. Bill is long, slender, and chisel-like**. Gray and black tail shows white patches near the corners. MALE: Has black crown and hindneck. FEMALE: Crown and hindneck are dark gray.

Similar Species: Red-breasted Nuthatch (p. 281) has rusty underparts. Pygmy Nuthatch (p. 285) is smaller, lacks black crown.

Voice: Common call is nasal *airrhh* or *eehr* and soft *ht, ht* notes; song is rapid series of rich *twhee, twhee* notes.

Where to Find: Uncommon to fairly common in open ponderosa pine and mixed forests, occasionally in oak woodlands. Does not occur in juniper stands or aspen groves.

Behavior: Acrobatic, creeping head-first down trunks and branches. Hammers at bark and seeds with wedge-tipped bill. Often seen in pairs or family groups. Nests in cavities in snags or live trees, using abandoned woodpecker nest holes.

Did you Know? Look and listen for this species where mature, open-spaced ponderosa pines occur. Outside of the breeding season, nuthatches often join multi-species chickadee feeding flocks.

Date and Location Seen: _____

_____

Description: 4.25″. Excitable, active little twittering nuthatch that feeds high in ponderosa pines. **Tiny**, with **grayish upperparts, buffy-white underparts** and grayish flanks. **Grayish-brown crown** is bordered by dark eye-line, whitish face and throat. Bill is relatively long and tail is short.

Similar Species: Larger White-breasted Nuthatch (p. 283) has a bright white face, rusty undertail. Larger Red-breasted Nuthatch (p. 281) has a distinct white eyebrow.

Voice: Call is high, rapid twittering *pip-pip-pip* notes, often given in chorus by a flock; also gives high chipping, squeaky notes.

Where to Find: Fairly common resident of dry, open mature ponderosa pine forests with snags. Somewhat more widespread in winter, but seldom far from ponderosa pines. Good areas include the forests around Sisters, Oregon; Spokane, Washington; National Bison Range, Montana; and Coeur d'Alene area, Idaho.

Behavior: Usually seen in flocks. Acrobatically forages for insects or pine seeds high in ponderosa pine tree branches. Gleans from foliage, probes bark crevices and cones, and scales off loose bark. Gregarious except when nesting, and often joins multi-species feeding flocks. Roosts and nests in tree cavities. Caches seeds.

Did you Know? One of the best ways to find Pygmy Nuthatches is to walk quietly through ponderosa pine forests listening for their diagnostic, high-pitched twittering calls, emanating from the tops of the trees.

Date and Location Seen: _____

_____

Description: 5.25″. **Tiny**, cryptic **trunk-creeping bird** with a long, thin **down-curved bill. Mottled brownish-gray** above with whitish eyebrow, long buffy wingstripe, and rusty rump; whitish below. Has long, stiff tail.

Similar Species: Nuthatches lack mottled-brown upperparts and down-curved bill.

Voice: Best recognized by very high, thin *tseeee* note; song is rhythmic *see-see-seee, seedly-see.*

Where to Find: Fairly common resident of mature coniferous and mixed forests. More widespread in winter. Some migratory movements noted (April-May, October-November).

Behavior: Forages for insects picked from tree bark crevices. Feeds by flying to the base of a tree and creeping upward, spiraling around the trunk until it reaches the top. Then it flies to the next tree and repeats the process. Builds nest under loose sections of tree bark. Frequently encountered in mixed species foraging flocks outside of the breeding season.

Did you Know? The mottled plumage of Brown Creepers strongly resembles conifer tree bark. When the bird senses danger it stops moving and relies upon its camouflaged coloration to help avoid detection.

Date and Location Seen: _____

_____

Rock Wren

Canyon Wren

Description: 6"/5.75". ROCK WREN: **Pale gray-brown** with **buff belly**. Back speckled with white; whitish **breast** is **finely streaked**; head has whitish eyebrow; tail is barred; bill is long, thin. CANYON WREN: Dark **rufous-brown back** with pale and dark spots; **rufous breast** with faint dark bars; **tail bright rufous** with thin, black barring; head pale and dark-spotted gray; **throat contrasting white. Bill very long**, thin, slightly decurved.

Similar Species: Bewick's Wren (p. 291) has conspicuous white eyebrow. House Wren (p. 291) is brown, barred with black.

Voice: ROCK WREN: Call is trilled *pidzeee* and *deee-dee*; song has buzzy, trilled phrases. CANYON WREN: Call is loud buzzy *jeep*; song is cascading series of clear whistles, falling and slowing down.

Where to Find: ROCK WREN: Common summer resident (April-October), rare in winter. Found mainly at open, sunny rock outcroppings, rockslides, and rocky fields. CANYON WREN: Fairly common resident of rocky cliffs and outcroppings.

Behavior: Both forage for insects and spiders almost exclusively on rocks, talus slopes. ROCK WREN: Prefers open, sunny areas, including rocky deserts. CANYON WREN: Favors cracks and crevices, with vertical rock walls or outcrops. Both build nests deep within rock crevices.

Did you Know? Rock Wrens often place many small pebbles at the entrance to their nest cavities. The function of these rocks is unknown.

Date and Location Seen: ───────────────

House Wren

Bewick's Wren

Description: 4.75"/5.25". HOUSE WREN: **Plain brownish** with **fine black barring** on wings, flanks, undertail, tail. Has thin, indistinct eyebrow. BEWICK'S WREN: **Brown above** with distinct **white eyebrow, grayish white below**. Undertail and upper surface of tail finely barred with black.

Similar Species: Smaller Winter Wren (p. 293) is all dark brown with short tail. Marsh Wren (p. 295) has striped back, shorter tail, with rusty wings and rump.

Voice: Extremely varied. HOUSE: Common calls include musical *jirrd* or mewing notes. Bubbly song consists of series of rattles and trills. BEWICK'S: Common calls include a scolding *bzzzzz*. Varied song has short introductory notes and buzzes that end in musical trill.

Where to Find: HOUSE: Common migrant and summer resident (April-September) of riparian areas, upland forests, and residential areas with open space and trees. BEWICK's: Fairly common or uncommon resident of low-elevation dense, brushy habitats in south-central, northern, and northeastern Oregon; southeastern Washington; and north-central and southeastern Idaho. Rare elsewhere. Range is expanding north and eastward; sightings are increasing.

Behavior: Both species glean insects from foliage in brushy areas. House Wrens prefer more open, dryer areas. Both nest in natural cavities, woodpecker nest holes, or constructed nest boxes.

Did you Know? Both species are strongly territorial, and will destroy the eggs of other wrens or songbirds nesting nearby.

Date and Location Seen: _____

_____

291

Description: 4". **Tiny**, shy waif of dark, brushy habitats. **Dark brown overall** with rufous-brown breast. Fine black barring on wings, flanks, and tail. **Short tail is usually cocked upward**. Has thin, indistinct buffy eyebrow.

Similar Species: Larger House Wren (p. 291) has paler underparts and longer tail.

Voice: Call is emphatic *jip-jip*; song is a long and complex series of high, thin tinkling trills.

Where to Find: Fairly common resident of dense, moist coniferous forests, usually riparian areas.

Behavior: Actively and methodically forages for insects and other invertebrates on the ground; typically in low shrubs, around logs, through brush piles, or under stream banks. Nests often built in natural cavities, usually in dead trees on or near the ground. Male sometimes builds numerous nests. Frequently moves downslope in fall to low-elevation brushy riparian woodlands.

Did you Know? The Winter Wren may be best appreciated for its incredibly complex and lovely, melodious songs. The birds that sing in our region produce an astounding average of 36 notes per second.

Date and Location Seen: _____

_____

Description: 5". Small, busy marsh denizen with dark crown, **whitish eyebrow, black and white striped back, rusty wings and rump**. Has a dull whitish breast with tan flanks and belly. **Short tail is held vertically**. Long, thin bill curves down. JUVENILE: Patterning more subdued than adult's.

Similar Species: Larger Bewick's Wren (p. 291) has bolder white eyebrow. House Wren (p. 291) is uniform plain brown with only a very faint eyebrow.

Voice: Call is hard *tek*; song is gurgling, rattling trill that begins with a few call notes.

Where to Find: Common migrant (April-May, September-October) and summer resident of marshes. Uncommon in winter, usually in lowland wetlands.

Behavior: Gleans for insects beneath dense cattail and bulrush cover. Often stays well hidden, but singing birds sometimes sit more openly. Male sings day or night. Nest is a woven structure attached to reeds.

Did you Know? A male Marsh Wren builds multiple nests for the female, and then she selects the one she finds most suitable.

Date and Location Seen: _____

_____

Description: 7.5". **Chunky, slate-gray** streamside bird with a **short tail**, thin, dark bill, and long legs. Frequently flashes white eyelids and **bobs** up and down.

Similar Species: Distinctive species; larger and darker than wrens.

Voice: Call is high, buzzy *dzeet*; song is series of high whistled or trilled phrases.

Where to Find: Fairly common residents of clear, fast mountain streams with cascades, riffles, and waterfalls. In late fall they move downstream to winter along lower elevation streams and rivers. Regularly seen along Icicle River, Washington; Wallowa River near Minam, Oregon; Rattlesnake Creek in Missoula, Montana; and upper Boise River near Boise, Idaho.

Behavior: Mainly forages for aquatic insects. Flies rapidly up and down streams, actively patrols for food or defends territory. Bobs on emergent rocks; swims, dives, or wades through the water, and often disappears for short periods below the surface. When underwater, strides along stream bottoms by rowing with powerful wings. Builds domed nest from moss along streamsides or under bridges.

Did you Know? American Dippers have specialized physiological adaptations that allow them to survive immersion in cold water.

Date and Location Seen: _____

_____

Golden-crowned Kinglet
Male

Ruby-crowned
Kinglet

Description: 4"/4.25". GOLDEN-CROWNED: **Tiny**, with olive-gray upperparts, grayish-white underparts, dark flight feathers with golden edging and **white wing-bars**. Tail is short and notched, bill is tiny and thin. Has broad **white eyebrow below black crown stripe**. Crown center is orange in male, golden-yellow in female. RUBY-CROWNED: Similar to Golden-crowned, but **olive overall with broken white eye-ring**. Male's bright red crest usually hidden unless bird is agitated. **Both species nervously flick wings**.

Similar Species: Warblers are larger than kinglets, and do not flick wings. Vireos are longer, more robust.

Voice: GOLDEN-CROWNED: Call is high, thin *tsee*. Song starts with high, thin notes, ends in tumbling series. RUBY-CROWNED: Call is husky, dry *ji-dit*. Song starts with high, thin descending notes that build into loud and warbled, repeated phrases.

Where to Find: GOLDEN-CROWNED: Common resident of low- to mid-elevation coniferous forests. RUBY-CROWNED: Fairly common summer resident of high-elevation coniferous forests, uncommon-rare in winter.

Behavior: Both species forage and nest in coniferous trees, feed by gleaning insects from tree and shrub branches. Gregarious, form post-breeding flocks. Often make downslope migrations in late fall to valleys, where they winter.

Did you Know? After the breeding season, kinglets, chickadees, and other species typically form feeding flocks or "guilds" that forage together through tree and shrub canopies in search of food.

Date and Location Seen: _____

_____

Western Bluebird
Male

Western Bluebird
Female

Mountain Bluebird
Male

Mountain Bluebird
Female

Description: 7". WESTERN: Plump thrush with a short tail and long pointed wings. **Blue head, wings, rump**, and **tail. Breast, sides, and variable patch on back are rusty brown**. Male's blue areas are deep and vibrant. Female's plumage is paler and more subdued. MOUNTAIN: Slimmer, longer-tailed and longer-winged than Western. Male is **overall sky blue**, with whitish belly and undertail. Female is light gray overall, with slight tan to buff wash on breast. Has pale blue wings and tail; white eye-ring.

Similar Species: Male Lazuli Bunting (p. 381) has bold white wing-bars, finch-like bill.

Voice: WESTERN: Call is musical *phew*. MOUNTAIN: Call is low *chur*.

Where to Find: WESTERN: Fairly common migrant (February-April, September-November) and summer resident of open coniferous forests and forest edge habitats. MOUNTAIN: Common migrant (February-March, September-October) and summer resident in varied open areas from low-elevation foothills to alpine meadows. Both species are uncommon to rare in winter.

Behavior: Both species capture insects using a variety of techniques; also feed on berries, especially in winter. Both are cavity-nesters, using natural holes in trees, old woodpecker holes, and man-made nest boxes.

Did you Know? Bluebird populations have benefited greatly from the installation of man-made nest boxes, mostly because of limited available nesting cavities and competition from other cavity nesters, especially European Starlings.

Date and Location Seen: _____

_____

Description: 8.5". Slim, cryptically-plumaged thrush of dry foothills and mountains. **Long-tailed** and short-billed. Overall **plain gray** with bold **white eye-ring**; buffy wing patch and **white tail sides** show in flight.

Similar Species: Northern Mockingbird (rare) lacks white eyering, has distinct white wing-bars and wing patches. Smaller female Mountain Bluebird (p. 301) has a much shorter tail, blue in wings and tail, and lacks buffy wing patch.

Voice: Call is soft, whistled *heeh*; song is long, finch-like warble.

Where to Find: Fairly common summer resident of dry, open coniferous forests. Common migrant and winter resident (October-April) primarily in juniper woodlands and other areas offering fruit and berries.

Behavior: Forages mainly for insects, other invertebrates, and berries in summer; feeds almost exclusively on juniper berries in winter. Flycatches and also gleans insects from foliage on the ground. Nests on or near the ground in cavities with overhanging cover, often in cut banks.

Did you Know? Townsend's Solitaires aggressively defend their winter territories in juniper habitats from other birds.

Date and Location Seen: _____

Description: 7". Medium-size thrush of montane riparian areas. **Upperparts** are **reddish-brown; breast is buffy with indistinct brown spots**, and belly is grayish-white.

Similar Species: Swainson's (p. 307) and Hermit Thrushes (p. 309) have prominent spotting on their breasts and lack reddish-brown backs.

Voice: Call is nasal *veer*; song is flute-like, descending *vree, vee-ur, vee-ur, veer, veer, veer, veer*.

Where to Find: Common summer resident (May-September) of low- to mid-elevation riparian areas with dense, shrubby habitats in Washington; the Blue Mountains of Oregon; and the northern half of Idaho and Montana.

Behavior: Forages mainly on the ground for insects and fruit. Nests on or near the ground in low shrubs. Shy, heard far more often than seen.

Did you Know? This shy, beautiful thrush is heard far more often than it is seen.

Date and Location Seen: _____

_____

Description: 7". *Catharus* thrushes are plump, thin-billed birds with spotted breasts and buffy wing stripes. Swainson's is **uniformly olive-brown** on the **upperparts, wings**, and **tail**. Has broad, **buff eye-ring; throat and breast** are **buffy with dark brown spots**; flanks are olive, belly is white.

Similar Species: Hermit Thrush (p. 309) has contrasting reddish tail, white eye-ring. Veery (p. 305) has rusty-brown upperparts and faint spots on creamy breast.

Voice: Call is low, liquid *quip*; song has fluty phrases that spiral upward.

Where to Find: Common migrant (May-June, August-September) and summer resident of low- to mid-elevation moist deciduous woodlands and coniferous forests with dense shrub understories, often in riparian areas.

Behavior: Feeds on insects and fruit deep within shady woodland understory, sometimes more openly on pathways or edges. Secretive, more often heard than seen.

Did you Know? Swainson's Thrushes migrate mainly at night, and their distinctive *queee* flight calls can be heard on quiet spring and fall evenings.

Date and Location Seen: _____

_____

Description: 6.75". Pale **brownish-gray above**, with **rump and tail contrastingly reddish brown**. Buffy-white on **breast with blackish spots**; sides and flanks are grayish, belly is white. Has complete, **thin, white eye-ring**.

Similar Species: Swainson's Thrush (p. 307) lacks reddish tail and has buffy face pattern. Veery (p. 305) has reddish-brown upperparts and indistinct brown spots on buffy breast. Neither flicks wings or tail.

Voice: Call is sharp *chup-chup*. Song begins with long whistle, then cascading fluty whistles; successive songs are on different pitches.

Where to Find: Common migrant (April-May, September-November) and summer resident in mid- to high-elevation mature coniferous forests. Rare in the Treasure Valley, Idaho and Columbia Basin, Washington in winter.

Behavior: Forages on the ground for insects, usually remaining in shade. Often visits fruiting shrubs. Usually seen singly. Rapidly flicks wings and slowly raises and lowers tail when perched.

Did you Know? Many birders consider this species the finest songster in North America.

Date and Location Seen: _____

_____

Male

Juvenile

Description: 10". Familiar large, plump thrush with gray-brown upperparts, **rufous-red breast, and white markings around the eyes**. MALE: Head blackish, breast deep reddish-orange. FEMALE: Paler, duller with gray-brown head. JUVENILE: Heavily spotted on the breast, whitish on wings and back.

Similar Species: Varied Thrush (p. 313) has long orange eye-brow, gray or black breast band, orange patterning on wings.

Voice: Song is pleasing carol of two- or three-note, rich whistled phrases. Calls include a hard *pup-pup*, a squealing *kli-kli-pup*, and a high lisping flight call.

Where to Find: Common migrant (February-March, September-October) and summer resident of moist woodlands and forests. In winter, they form flocks that wander widely in search of food sources.

Behavior: In summer, feeds mainly on the ground for earthworms and grubs. Winter flocks seek berries and fruit; often joining flocks of waxwings. Nest is a mud-lined open cup, usually placed in a crotch of a tree, but also on or in human structures where there is overhead protection.

Did you Know? Robins ground forage by making short, fast, and halting runs to find worms and other prey. Occasionally the bird stops, cocks its head, and then pounces on a worm. Although it appears that robins are listening for their subterranean prey, a study in 1965 proved that they actually locate worms by sight.

Date and Location Seen: _____

_____

Male

Female

Description: 9.5". **Robin-like** thrush of mature, moist coniferous forests. Has **dark breast band, mask**, and **bill**; **orange eyebrow**, throat, wing patches and wing-bars. MALE: Has **bluish-gray** head, back, and tail; black mask and breast band. FEMALE: Faded version of male, with grayish upperparts and faded breast band.

Similar Species: American Robin (p. 311) has no breast band, eyebrow or orange wing patches.

Voice: Call is deep *chup*. Song is single, long whistle on one pitch followed every ten seconds by another note on a different pitch.

Where to Find: Fairly common summer resident (March-October) of moist coniferous forests, mostly at mid- to high-elevations. Rare in winter.

Behavior: Mostly forages through forest litter on the ground for insects and other invertebrates, also feeds on seeds and berries. Shy, most often seen in dark, shadowy habitats. Moves downslope in fall to winter in low-elevation riparian and coniferous forests. Occasionally wanders to the Midwest and East Coast.

Did you Know? The eerie, beautiful song of Varied Thrushes can be heard most often in early morning, late evening, and after a rain shower.

Date and Location Seen: _____

_____

Description: 8.5". A **slate-gray bird** with a black crown. Has long, black tail and **rufous undertail**.

Similar Species: Very distinctive; no other species is uniform slate-gray.

Voice: Call is hoarse, catlike mewing. Song is rambling, halting series of melodious, nasal, and squeaky notes and phrases interspersed with catlike *mew* notes.

Where to Find: Locally common summer resident (May-September) of dense riparian woodlands. Ranges from Montana and Idaho westward through the Blue Mountains of Washington, locally to central Oregon. Rare elsewhere.

Behavior: Forages mainly on the ground or low in very dense thickets for insects, seeds, and small fruits. Flight is typically low. Avoids crossing large openings and stays hidden in dense cover. Rises to a tall perch only to sing. Recognizes cowbird eggs and will eject them from the nest.

Did you Know? Gray Catbird is an expert mimic and often incorporates the calls and songs of other birds into its song.

Date and Location Seen: _____

Description: 8.5″. Medium-size, **long-tailed** songbird of sage-brush country. **Upperparts light grayish-brown** with two fine, white wing-bars; **underparts whitish with crisp, dark streaking**; head has indistinct whitish eye-line and short, straight bill; tail is brownish gray with white corners.

Similar Species: Northern Mockingbird (rare) lacks crisp, dark streaking on underparts, has large white wing patches.

Voice: Call is low *chup*; song is long, clear series of warbled phrases.

Where to Find: Fairly common migrant (March-May, July-September) and summer resident of sagebrush rangelands.

Behavior: Forages on the ground mostly for insects and other invertebrates, also eats berries if available. Builds its stick nest on or close to the ground in sagebrush. Sometimes builds shade platform over the nest.

Did you Know? When threatened by an intruder, Sage Thrashers escape by dropping to the ground and running, usually maintaining sufficient visual cover between themselves and their intruder.

Date and Location Seen: _____

Breeding Female

Non-breeding

Juvenile

Description: 8.5". Stocky, **blackish** songbird with **short, squared tail** and pointed, brown wings. Has **straight, pointed bill**; dull pinkish-orange legs. BREEDING: Body plumage **iridescent black, bill bright yellow**. WINTER: Plumage **heavily spangled with whitish** spots, bill blackish; white spotting wears away in late winter to reveal breeding plumage. JUVENILE: Gray-brown throughout, with dark bill and lores, but shows distinctive starling shape.

Similar Species: Brewer's Blackbird (p. 391) has longer tail, pale yellow eyes, and is unspotted.

Voice: Calls include a buzzy *dzeeer*, harsh *shurrr*, and sharp *vit*. Extremely varied songs incorporate much mimicry. Buzzes, clicks, rattles, and high squealing characterize the prolonged song.

Where to Find: Common resident of open areas containing trees or buildings, especially in agricultural and residential areas. Gathers into large post-breeding season foraging flocks.

Behavior: Waddles on ground, using gaping motion of bill to probe lawns and soil. Flocks also exploit fruit, grain, and insects. Flies with rapid wingbeats, flight silhouette appearing triangular. Nests in trees or structure cavities, often aggressively usurping other nesting species. Forms large post-breeding feeding flocks that can number in the thousands.

Did you Know? This non-native species was introduced from Europe to New York in the late 1800s. As mimics, they imitate many other birds and sounds they hear.

Date and Location Seen: _____

Non-breeding

Description: 6.5". Slender ground bird with a **thin bill**, gray-brown upperparts, pale, **buff-tinged underparts with streaks on the breast**, and **white outer tail feathers**. BREEDING: Grayer above and richer buff below, with breast streaks reduced or absent. WINTER: More heavily streaked below, faintly streaked on back.

Similar Species: Larger Horned Lark (p. 261) has a black mask and throat and white-edged black tail. Many sparrows are somewhat similar, but have short, conical bills and do not bob tails.

Voice: Calls include thin *tseep* and doubled *tsi-sip*.

Where to Find: Common migrant (April-May, August-October) in open lowland areas. Fairly common summer resident of mountain alpine areas. Rare in winter, mainly along the lower Columbia Basin.

Behavior: Diet is mostly insects and some seeds. Walks on the ground, constantly bobbing tail. Post-breeding flocks forage in open fields, sometimes mixing with Horned Larks. Usually seen on the ground, but also perches on fence lines, wires, tree branches. Nests on ground in wet alpine areas with scattered rocks. Moves to lower elevations after nesting; forms large flocks in migration. Migrants prefer moist areas; often found on receding shorelines and meadowlands.

Did you Know? Males make interesting courtship flights. They fly up high in the air and then float downward while singing, holding their legs extended and tails cocked upward.

Date and Location Seen: _____

_____

Cedar Waxwing
Adult

Cedar Waxwing
Juvenile

Bohemian Waxwing

Bohemian Waxwing

Description: 7.25"/8.25". **Crested** birds that travel in close flocks. CEDAR: **Soft brown, tinged yellow on belly; black chin and mask**; lower back and rump gray. Blackish tail has **yellow band** at tip. Some have small, wax-like red spots on tips of inner flight feathers. BOHEMIAN: Similar to Cedar, but **larger and grayer**; has **grayish belly** and **rufous undertail**. **Wings have distinct yellow and white markings**.

Similar Species: European Starlings (p. 319) have similar flocking behavior and triangular flight shape, but different markings.

Voice: CEDAR: Call is very high *sreeee*. BOHEMIAN: Call is like Cedar's, but lower-pitched and trilled.

Where to Find: CEDAR: Common residents of low-elevation valleys, including residential areas. BOHEMIAN: Uncommon to common and irregular winter residents (November-April) of valleys, found wherever plentiful sources of fruit exist. Seen most winters in Brewster and Spokane, Washington; Joseph and Enterprise, Oregon.

Behavior: Both species share similar habits and often occur together. Gather in large flocks when not nesting and concentrate at prime foraging areas. Diet is mainly insects in summer, fruit and berries in fall and winter. Flocks often visit holly, juniper, mountain ash, and many other fruit-bearing ornamental plantings.

Did you Know? Fruit-bearing shrubs and trees are essential to the survival of waxwings.

Date and Location Seen: _____

_____

Description: 5". **Plain olive-yellow throughout**; with indistinct eyebrow, **yellowish eye-ring broken by thin, dark line through eye**; faint **olive breast streaking** and olive-gray tail. MALE: Has dull orange crown patch, usually hidden; and body plumage is brighter yellow-olive. FEMALE: Has duller plumage; head tinged grayish in some birds.

Similar Species: Yellow Warbler (p. 329) lacks dark eyeline; has shorter tail with pale yellow areas, and pale yellow edges to wing feathers. Tennessee Warbler (rare) is very similar, but has whitish undertail coverts and pale eyeline.

Voice: Call is sharp *tik*; song is colorless trill that usually rises, and then falls slightly in pitch.

Where to Find: Common migrant and summer resident (April-September) in dense, brushy areas of deciduous and mixed woodlands, including aspen and mountain mahogany. Rare in winter, mainly in the lower Columbia Basin and southwest Idaho.

Behavior: Gleans and probes foliage for insects; often feeds low in shrubs. Nests on or near the ground.

Did you Know? This species is divided into four subspecies that differ in plumage color, size, and molt patterns. Of the four subspecies, it is likely that three visit or nest in our region.

Date and Location Seen: _____

_____

Nashville Warbler
Male

Virginia's Warbler

Description: 4.75". Small, relatively short-tailed warblers that have a **complete white eye-ring** on a **gray head**, and **yellow tail coverts**. Males have a distinctive blue-gray head that includes a (often hidden) rufous crown patch. NASHVILLE: **Olive upperparts**, mostly **yellow underparts including throat**. VIRGINIA'S: Male is **gray overall** with **yellow breast** and **tail coverts**. Female and immature duller.

Similar Species: MacGillivray's Warbler (p 339) has a gray hood and broken white eye-ring.

Voice: Both give a sharp *spink* call. NASHVILLE: Song is series of *seepa* notes followed by a short trill. VIRGINIA'S: Call and song very similar to Nashville's.

Where to Find: NASHVILLE: Common migrant (April-May, July-September), common in summer in low- to mid-elevation dry coniferous and mixed forests with dense shrub understories. Often seen in shrubby clearcuts and riparian areas. VIRGINIA'S: Uncommon and local breeder in southeastern Idaho associated with brushy or riparian areas in juniper forests. May be seen at Mink Creek, near Pocatello, Idaho.

Behavior: Both frequently bob their tails up and down while foraging. Glean for insects and spiders in foliage of low shrubs and trees. Typical of warblers, males on territory may sing for many minutes from a high perch.

Did you Know? The Nashville species scientific name *ruficapilla* refers to the hidden rufous crown patch of males.

Date and Location Seen: _____

_____

Male

Female

Description: 5″. Fairly stocky, **short-tailed** warbler that is **mainly yellow throughout**. Plain head lacks markings except for a **bold, dark eye** and indistinct pale eye-ring. MALE: Bright yellow, with **thin red streaks on the breast**. FEMALE: Duller, paler, and lacking red streaks. Immature females can be very dull, nearly lacking yellow. All birds show yellow patches in tail (**tail appears all yellow below**), yellow or whitish edges to wing feathers.

Similar Species: Orange-crowned (p. 325) and Wilson's Warblers (p. 343) have longer, all dark tails.

Voice: Call is loud, down-slurred *chip*; sprightly song starts with high *sweet* notes, then a short twitter and an emphatic ending *see-see-whew*.

Where to Find: Common migrant (April-May, August-September) and summer resident of brushy riparian woodlands and thickets.

Behavior: Employs typical warbler gleaning behavior while foraging for insects, sometimes high in deciduous trees. Forms fairly large flocks during migration, when it often uses more varied habitats. Nest is built low in a bush or small tree.

Did you Know? As with many of our riparian species, Yellow Warbler nests are often parasitized by Brown-headed Cowbirds, but the warbler can recognize cowbird eggs and re-nest.

Date and Location Seen: _____

_____

Audubon's Breeding Male

Audubon's Non-breeding

Myrtle Non-breeding

Audubon's Immature Female

Description: 5.5" Our most abundant warbler has **bright yellow rump patch, yellow patch on sides**, and **white tail spots**. Gray to gray-brown, with white wing-bars and whitish belly. "Audubon's" subspecies has **yellow throat patch** (may be whitish in immature females); breeding male has black chest, large white wing patch. "Myrtle" subspecies has white throat which extends back to point behind ear region and then whitish eyebrow; breeding male has mottled black chest and bold white wing-bars.

Similar Species: Yellow rump patch distinguishes even the dullest immatures from other regularly seen warblers.

Voice: "Audubon's" call is loud *chip* and "Myrtle" gives a flatter *chep*; song is loosely patterned warble.

Where to Find: Common and widespread migrants (March-May, August-October). Uncommon in winter in lower Columbia Basin and southwestern Idaho; rare elsewhere. "Audubon's" is common summer resident of open, dry coniferous forests and mixed woodlands, with considerable ground foliage. "Myrtle" is uncommon to rare migrant and winter resident.

Behavior: Feeds by gleaning foliage, flycatching, hovering, or searching on the ground. Diet is mainly insects, but also includes fruit. Noted as one of the last warblers to leave their breeding grounds in fall, and one of the first to return in spring. Often forages in large flocks in migration.

Did you Know? The "Audubon's" and "Myrtle" subspecies were formerly regarded as separate species.

Date and Location Seen: _____

_____

Male

Female Immature

Description: 5". **Gray above** and **white below**, with black markings and much white in outer tail feathers. Dark ear patch connects to gray hind-neck; has two **white wing-bars. Tiny yellow spot in front of the eye** may be difficult to see. MALE: **Black ear patch and throat**, with **bold, black streaks on the sides**. FEMALE: Dark gray ear patch, some black on lower throat; immature female lacks black on throat.

Similar Species: Townsend's Warbler (p. 335) has extensive olive and yellow coloration. Mountain Chickadees lack (p. 277) streaked sides, wing-bars, yellow eye spot, and have a white ear patch.

Voice: Call is dull *tup*; song is series of high, buzzy notes, e.g. *zeea-zeea-zeea-ZEE-zee*.

Where to Find: Uncommon migrant and summer resident (May-September) in open coniferous and mixed forests, especially juniper forests with shrub understories. Most abundant in Klickitat and Yakima Counties, Washington; Hood River and Wasco Counties, Oregon; and southern Oregon and Idaho. Rare elsewhere in the region.

Behavior: Actively gleans insects from shrubs and trees. During migration, often seen in mixed feeding flocks in a variety of semi-open habitats, especially riparian areas.

Did you Know? The Black-throated Gray Warbler is considered a short-distance migrant, moving from its breeding areas in the western United States only as far south as Mexico.

Date and Location Seen: _____

_____

Male

Female

Description: 5". Distinctive warbler of tall, moist conifers. Exhibits **yellow and dark head pattern** with **yellow arc below eye, yellow breast with dark flank streaking**, olive-green upperparts, dark wings with two bold white wing-bars, white belly. MALE: Has black on the throat, ear patch, and much of the crown. Immature males are similar but have less black. FEMALE: Has olive-green ear patch and crown with little black on the throat. The dullest females lack black throats and are pale yellow on the throat and breast.

Similar Species: Black-throated Gray Warbler (p. 333) is similar, but is white instead of yellow on the face and breast. Hermit Warbler (rare) lacks yellow on the breast and flank streaking.

Voice: Call is high *tip*; typical song is rising, buzzy *zee zee zee zee zeeeeee zeeta-zee.*

Where to Find: Common migrant (May-June, August-October), summer resident of mature mid-elevation coniferous forests.

Behavior: Actively gleans, hover-gleans, and flycatches insects in the upper portion of tree canopy. Males sing from the tops of tall trees. Joins mixed species flocks in migration.

Did you Know? Townsend's Warblers occur along the eastern slopes of the Cascades where they frequently interbreed with the related Hermit Warbler.

Date and Location Seen: _____

_____

Male

Female

Description: 5.25". Small, distinctive and energetic warbler. MALE: **Head, back, and breast are entirely black. Wings are black with bold orange wing-bars** and underwings. Tail is long and **black with orange base**. Belly is white. Bill is short. FEMALE: Patterned like male, but black is replaced by light gray on head, back is light gray to green. Sides, wing-bars, and tail base are yellow.

Similar Species: Unmistakable.

Voice: Call is high *tsip*; songs variable, but include a high *tsee tsee tsee tsee tsee tsee tswee* and *teetsa teetsa teetsa teetsa seet*.

Where to Find: Rare to fairly common migrant (May-June, August-September) and summer resident of the Rockies and mountains of northern Washington; rare and irregular in the Blue and Cascade Mountains. Favors moist, deciduous forest, often second-growth, with abundant shrubs. Most often seen in riparian areas. Breeds at Coppei Creek, Washington; Upper Umatilla River, Oregon; Hoodoo Valley, Idaho; and near Seeley Lake, Montana.

Behavior: Diet is mainly insects caught by gleaning and flycatching. An acrobatic and lively feeder, they frequently flash their wing and tail patches when foraging. Nest is placed low in fork of small shrub or tree.

Did you Know? It is thought that redstarts flash their wing and tail patches when foraging in order to flush insects that are hidden in the foliage.

Date and Location Seen: _____

_____

Male

Description: 5.25". Skulking warbler of dense thickets. **Olive-green above** and **yellow below. Head, throat, and breast are mostly gray** (appears **dark hooded**) with **prominent white arcs above and below the eyes**. Bill is relatively long and bi-colored (blackish above, pinkish below) and legs are long and pinkish. MALE: Hood is dark gray, darkest in front of eyes and across breast. FEMALE, IMMATURE: Hood is pale gray, lightest (sometimes whitish) on throat.

Similar Species: Nashville Warbler (p. 327) has yellow throat and complete eye-ring. Orange-crowned Warbler (p. 325) lacks defined gray hood, has blurry breast streaking.

Voice: Call is hard, sharp *chik*; song is short series *swee-swee-swee-swee, sweet.*

Where to Find: Fairly common migrant (May-June, August-September) and summer resident of mid- to high-elevation riparian and brushy areas.

Behavior: Gleans for insects close to the ground in moist, dense shrubby places, mainly riparian areas and cutover forests.

Did you Know? This species had originally been called Tolmie's Warbler by John Kirk Townsend in honor of Dr. W.T. Tolmie, the surgeon at Fort Vancouver, Washington. It was re-named MacGillivray's Warbler by John James Audubon in honor of his Scottish editor Dr. William MacGillivray.

Date and Location Seen: _____

_____

Male

Female

Description: 5". A skulking, masked, marsh-dwelling warbler. **Bright yellow throat** contrasts with duller **flanks washed with brownish**. Upperparts olive-green; undertail yellow. MALE: **Bold black mask and forehead** bordered behind by white. FEMALE: Lacks mask, has indistinct whitish eye-ring; pale yellow throat contrasts with brownish cheeks and flanks. Young males have faint black face mask.

Similar Species: Female Yellow (p. 329), Nashville (p. 327), Orange-crowned (p. 325), and MacGillivray's Warblers (p. 339) are similar, but lack Yellowthroat's strong contrast between pale yellow throat and dull, pale brownish underparts, and indistinct complete eye-ring.

Voice: Call is husky *tidge*; distinctive, loud song is *wich-i-ty wich-i-ty wich-i-ty*.

Where to Find: Common migrant and summer resident (April-September) of marshes, wet meadows, and other wetlands with dense, emergent vegetation, usually cattails. Migrants often use dense, brushy habitats.

Behavior: Gleans insects and spiders in cattails, bulrushes, or dense shrubby vegetation. Male sings from an open perch, and sometimes gives song in short flights. Builds loose, bulky nest on or near the ground.

Did you Know? Along with Yellow Warbler, this is the most widespread warbler in North America.

Date and Location Seen: _____

_____

Male

Female

Description: 4.75". A small, active warbler that is **bright yellow-olive above** and **bright golden-yellow below**. The yellow forehead contrasts with a **shiny black crown** (males) or mixed black and olive crown in most females (some females show only olive). The dark eye stands out on the blank yellow face. The wings and tail are unmarked olive-green.

Similar Species: Yellow Warbler (p. 329) is plumper and shorter tailed, has yellow tail spots and edges to wing feathers. Orange-crowned Warbler (p. 325) is much duller olive-yellow overall and has yellowish eye-ring broken by thin dark line through the eye.

Voice: Call is distinctive, soft *timp*. Song is rapid series of *chip* notes, building in volume and speed, but often trailing off at the end.

Where to Find: Common migrant (April-May, August-September) and summer resident of mid- to high-elevation coniferous forests with shrub thickets in riparian and wet areas. Rare in winter.

Behavior: Intensely active, gleaning, hovering, and making short sallies for flying insects, mostly close to the ground. The tail is flipped as the bird flits about. Nests on or near the ground in dense understory vegetation.

Did you Know? Along with the phalarope, snipe, plover, and storm-petrel, this is one of the birds named for famed late 18th and early 19th century American ornithologist Alexander Wilson.

Date and Location Seen: _____

_____

Description: 7.5″. **Large, thick-billed** warbler-like bird with **deep yellow throat and breast, white spectacle** around the eyes, olive upperparts, whitish belly, and a long olive tail. The sexes are similar, but females have less black in front of eye and less intensely yellow breast.

Similar Species: Common Yellowthroat (p. 341) is much smaller and lacks white spectacles.

Voice: Call is nasal *airrh* and a snappy *cheew*. Loud, rich song is distinctive, consisting of loose collection of chatters, rattles, caws, and whistles with notes sometimes repeated rapidly.

Where to Find: Uncommon and local migrant and summer resident (April-September) of dense riparian thickets in low-elevation valleys. Inconspicuous in migration.

Behavior: Skulks, sings, and forages in dense shrubs and thickets. Territorial male sometimes perches openly for pro-longed periods while singing, or sings exuberantly in flight with deep wingbeats. Feeds on insects and berries.

Did you Know? The relationship of Yellow-breasted Chats to other wood-warblers continues to be studied and debated. It now appears that this species is only distantly related to our more typical warblers.

Date and Location Seen: _____

_____

Breeding Adult
Male

Female

Description: 7.25". **Bill** is **stout** compared to slender, pointed bills of orioles, but not conical like those of grosbeaks. MALE: Has red to **orange-red head**; otherwise **bright yellow** with **black back, wings and tail**, two wing-bars (front yellow, rear white). FEMALE: Olive-green to olive-gray above, pale yellow below, with **two white wing-bars**; some show only limited yellow on underparts. Immature males have limited orange on face.

Similar Species: Female Bullock's Oriole (p. 395) has thinner, more pointed, darker bill.

Voice: Call is rising *pr-d-dik*; song is series of hoarse, scratchy robin-like phrases: *pr-rit, pre-ur-rit, pree-u*.

Where to Find: Common migrant (May-June, July-September) and summer resident of open coniferous and mixed forests.

Behavior: Gleans insects with sluggish movements through foliage, often high in trees; also sallies after flying insects.

Did you Know? DNA studies suggest that our tanagers are more closely related to our grosbeaks and buntings than to the diverse tanagers of the New World tropics.

Date and Location Seen: _____

_____

Green-tailed
Towhee

Spotted Towhee
Male

Spotted Towhee
Female

Description: 7.25"/ 8.5". GREEN-TAILED: Large sparrow with olive upperparts, **reddish cap, white throat, gray underparts**, and **green-tinged wings and tail**. SPOTTED: Large sparrow with **black hood, white-spotted black wings** and back, and white corners on black tail. Bright **rufous sides**, flanks, and undertail, contrasting with white center breast and belly. **Eyes are red**. Female is slightly duller, with slaty head. Juvenile is brownish and heavily streaked, has distinctive wing spotting and white tail corners.

Similar Species: Dark-eyed Junco (p. 375) is smaller, lacks white spots and rufous sides. Smaller size, lack of white tail corners separate streaked sparrows from juvenile towhee.

Voice: GREEN-TAILED: Call is mewing *meewe*. Song variable; a typical trill is *tip seeo see tweeeee chchchch*. SPOTTED: Call is harsh, rising mew *hreee-eee*. Song is loud, buzzy trill *che zheeeeee*.

Where to Find: GREEN-TAILED: A fairly common migrant and summer resident (April-September) of dry, dense desert shrub habitats, usually where junipers or mountain-mahogany are present. SPOTTED: Common summer resident of dense, moist shrubs, mainly in riparian woodlands. Fairly common in winter in lowland riparian habitats.

Behavior: Both species nest and forage in dense, brushy areas.

Did you Know? Towhees employ "double scratch" foraging, a quick one-hop forward, one-hop backward maneuver that turns over leaves and other ground debris to expose hidden food items.

Date and Location Seen: _____

Description: 6.25″. **Long-tailed**, round-headed wintering sparrow of open country. Has gray head with a **rufous crown** and eye-line. Upperparts are streaked rusty-brown with two **white wing-bars**. Underparts are pale gray with a **prominent dark central breast spot** and buff sides. Upper bill is dark gray, lower is yellow.

Similar Species: Larger immature White-crowned Sparrow (p. 371) lacks a central breast spot. Chipping Sparrow (p. 353) lacks a breast spot, has white line over the eye.

Voice: Call is clear, soft *tseet* and *tsidle-eet*.

Where to Find: Uncommon and local winter (October-March) resident. Numbers highly variable from year to year. Regularly winter in the Grande Ronde and Wallowa Valleys, Oregon; Ted Trueblood W.M.A., Idaho; Ninepipe N.W.R., Montana; and Columbia N.W.R., Washington.

Behavior: Forages mainly for seeds and invertebrates in willow riparian areas, brushy roadsides, fields, and hedgerows. Regularly perches on fencelines and small trees, but seldom high off the ground. Usually seen in small post-breeding flocks.

Did you Know? Wintering American Tree Sparrows are usually very sparsely distributed, but once found they show little fear of humans.

Date and Location Seen: _____

_____

Breeding

Juvenile

Description: 5.5". Small, slim, long-tailed sparrow with gray underparts and rump, and streaked brown back. BREEDING: Distinctive face pattern: **black eye-line, white eyebrow**, and **rufous crown**; bill is black. NON-BREEDING: Crown is finely-streaked and brownish, bill is dull pinkish. Juvenile is like dull non-breeding adult, but extensively streaked below.

Similar Species: Brewer's Sparrow (p. 355) has finely-streaked crown, pale area between bill and eye, and thin white eye-ring. American Tree Sparrow (p. 351) has a central breast spot.

Voice: Call includes rich *tseet* and soft *tik*. Song is dry trill, faster and less musical than similar song of Dark-eyed Junco.

Where to Find: Common migrant (April-May, August-October) and summer resident of dry, open coniferous forests. Rare in winter.

Behavior: Mainly forages for small seeds, fruits, and insects on the ground in grassy forest understory. Sings from elevated perch, and flies into trees when disturbed. Nests on the ground or low in small shrub or tree. Forms flocks in migration, often with other sparrow species.

Did you Know? They are among the most widespread sparrows in North America, breeding from Alaska to Nicaragua.

Date and Location Seen: _____

_____

Description: 5.5". Slender, pale, **long-tailed** sparrow with **finely streaked crown, narrow whitish eye-ring**, streaked grayish-brown upperparts, and **unstreaked pale-gray lowerparts**.

Similar Species: Immature Chipping Sparrow (p. 353) is darker, with strong dark eye-line, gray nape and rump.

Voice: Call is thin *tsip*; song is long, distinctive, descending series of buzzy trills.

Where to Find: Common to locally rare migrant (April-June, August-September) and summer resident of sagebrush desert and other shrublands of southeastern Oregon, southern Idaho, Columbia Basin and other areas where open shrublands occur.

Behavior: Forages on the ground and in low shrubs for insects and seeds. Can survive for extended period of time without supplemental water by obtaining moisture from food. Defends territories from low perches on shrubs. When approached by human intruders or predators, often escapes by scurrying away along the ground while calling. Builds nest low in shrubs or on the ground at the base of a shrub. Gregarious, usually found in flocks after the breeding season.

Did you Know? Brewer's Sparrow is typically the most abundant bird of sagebrush areas. Its long, buzzy song may be heard throughout the day and often into the night.

Date and Location Seen: _____

_____

ME!# VESPER SPARROW
Pooecetes gramineus

Description: 6.25". Common, **fairly large**, streaky sparrow of open areas. Upperparts are entirely dark-streaked grayish-brown and underparts are creamy-white with **fine dark streaks on the breast** (forming **central breast spot**) and flanks. **Has unstreaked belly** and **white outer tail feathers** visible in flight. Head patterned brown and tan; shows thin **white eye-ring. Small chestnut patch at bend of wing** is not always visible.

Similar Species: Savannah Sparrow (p. 363) has distinct eyebrow, lacks eye-ring, and has broad streaking on the flanks. Lapland Longspur (p. 377) has broad chestnut wing patch and bold eyebrow.

Voice: Call is sharp *chirp*; song consists of two pairs of low, slurred whistles followed by series of short, descending trills.

Where to Find: Uncommon to common migrant (April-May, August-September) and summer resident of dry, open grasslands, pastures, and sagebrush.

Behavior: Forages mainly for seeds and insects on the ground. Males sing from highest exposed perch in their territories, often fence posts or tall shrubs. Breeding males also give short flight songs. Migrates in small flocks.

Did you Know? When they feel threatened, female Vesper Sparrows pretend they are injured and scurry away from their nests dragging a wing to lure the intruder away.

Date and Location Seen: _____

_____

Adult

Description: 6.5". Large, handsomely-marked sparrow of open, arid country. **Bold face pattern** includes chestnut ear patch with white spot at rear, black "whiskers", white markings around eyes, and chestnut and white crown stripes. Whitish below with **black spot in center of breast**. Long, **rounded tail has bold white outer edge and corners**. IMMATURE: Slightly duller on head.

Similar Species: Smaller Chipping Sparrow (p. 353) has red crown, lacks face pattern and breast spot. Vesper Sparrow (p. 357) lacks bold chestnut and white head pattern, has eye-ring and streaked breast. Has white only on edges of tail.

Voice: Call is sharp warbler-like *tsip*. Song consists of varied short phrases, often repeated two to four times and includes sweet notes and rough, burry trills.

Where to Find: Fairly common migrant (March-May, July-September) and summer resident of lower elevation open areas, usually edges between grasslands and shrub lands, degraded sagebrush areas, or in open forests.

Behavior: Feeds on insects and seeds in short-grass areas. Flies with strong, undulating wingbeats. Has elaborate courtship display and nests on the ground or in small shrubs. Forms small family flocks in late summer that often join other sparrow species in feeding flocks.

Did you Know? The "harlequin" head pattern and brown, black, and white tail suggest some species of lark, but this bird is a true sparrow.

Date and Location Seen: _____

_____

Sage Sparrow
Adult

Black-throated Sparrow
Adult

Description: 6"/5.5". Distinctive sparrows of sagebrush country. SAGE: Medium-size sparrow with streaked brownish upperparts, **gray head with white and black moustache stripes**, white spot in front of eye, thin white eye-ring, **long white-edged black tail**. Underparts show **white breast with dark central breast spot**, streaked flanks. BLACK-THROATED: All-gray upperparts. **Black face** framed by **bold, white eyebrow and moustache stripe**, dark crown. Underparts pale with **distinct black throat**. Black tail has white corners.

Similar Species: Distinctive.

Voice: SAGE: Call is high, weak *tip*; song has hoarse phrases with little pitch change. BLACK-THROATED: Call is bell-like *tip*; song is short series of high, weak tinkling notes.

Where to Find: SAGE: Fairly common but local migrant and summer resident (February-October) of low-elevation sagebrush desert. Rare in winter. BLACK-THROATED: Uncommon and local migrant and summer resident (April-August) of very dry, rocky slopes with sagebrush and other desert shrubs in southern Oregon and Idaho. Rare and local in Columbia Basin. Populations variable from year to year.

Behavior: Both forage for insects and seeds on the ground and in shrubs. Both males sing from tops of shrubs, and both species construct nests in or under desert shrubs.

Did you Know? Black-throated Sparrows survive in desert environments without supplemental water due to their ability to utilize moisture from the foods they eat.

Date and Location Seen: _____

_____

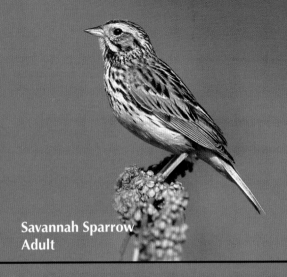

Savannah Sparrow
Adult

Grasshopper Sparrow

Description: 5.5"/ 5". SAVANNAH: **Small** sparrow of open areas, with **streaked** back, **breast**, and **flanks**; often has yellowish or white eyebrow. Has small bill, **short, notched tail**, and **bright pink legs.** GRASSHOPPER: **Unstreaked buffy below**, streaked rufous and brown above. Has relatively **large, flat head; eyebrow** that is **orangish in front, gray behind; dark crown with pale central stripe; long bill;** and short tail.

Similar Species: Song Sparrow (p. 367) has longer, rounded tail and grayer face.

Voice: SAVANNAH: Call is high, sharp *tick*; song is high *sip sip sip tseeeeeeee sirrrr.* GRASSHOPPER: Call is very high, sharp *tipip*; song is high, insect-like *tip tup seeeeeeeeee.*

Where to Find: SAVANNAH: Common migrant (April-May, August-September) and summer resident of open grassy areas, rare in winter. GRASSHOPPER: Uncommon and declining summer resident (April-September) of tall-grass hillsides with elevated perches. Reliable sites include National Bison Range, Montana; Midvale, Idaho area; and grasslands of northern Umatilla County, Oregon.

Behavior: Both species forage for insects and seeds, and nest on the ground. Savannah Sparrows often form large flocks in migration. Grasshopper Sparrows are loosely colonial.

Did you Know? Grasshopper Sparrows escape intruders by scurrying through the grass like mice, flying only when necessary.

Date and Location Seen: _____

_____

Description: 7". Large, stocky sparrow with a **gray head** and upperparts; **rusty wings and tail**; coarse, dark flank streaking, and white **breast with spots like inverted "Vs" or chevrons**.

Similar Species: Much smaller Song Sparrow (p. 367) has bold face pattern and streaked back.

Voice: Call is metallic *chink*; song is clear, ringing, and buzzy.

Where to Find: Fairly common migrant (April-May, August-October) and summer resident of dense shrub fields, open coniferous forests and riparian woodlands with heavy shrub understories at mid- to high-elevations. Rare in winter. Isolated populations breed in high desert mountain ranges in southwest Idaho and southeastern Oregon.

Behavior: Scratches on the ground for seeds and insects. Builds nest on the ground or in a low shrub.

Did you Know? Four distinct groups of Fox Sparrows have been recognized across their extensive breeding range, and some experts consider these four to be separate species. "Slate-colored" and "Thick-billed" groups nest in our region and have almost identical plumages, differing mainly by Thick-billed's massive bill. The coastal "Sooty" group is uniformly dark brown. The boreal "Red" Fox Sparrows, rare in our region, are rufous overall with a gray pattern on the face and gray streaks on the back.

Date and Location Seen: _____

_____

Description: 6.25″. Common and familiar long-tailed sparrow of wet, brushy areas. **Boldly streaked below**, with a blackish **central breast spot**. Strongly patterned face with **broad, gray eyebrow** and black whisker stripe. The **wings and tail are tinged rusty**. JUVENILE: More lightly streaked, with buffy wash below.

Similar Species: Much larger Fox Sparrow (p. 365) lacks bold face pattern and streaked back. Smaller Lincoln's Sparrow (p. 369) is less boldly streaked and has buffy breast. Savannah Sparrow (p. 363) is smaller, has short, notched tail, bright pink legs, and usually has yellowish eyebrow.

Voice: Call is distinctive *chimp*; song is variable series of trills following several short, sharp notes.

Where to Find: Common resident of low-elevation riparian woodlands, and other wet, densely-vegetated habitats, including residential areas.

Behavior: Diet is varied, but consists mostly of insects, seeds, and berries. Singing males may perch openly for many minutes, but otherwise they forage low, often on the ground. Nests on the ground or low in a shrub.

Did you Know? Over two dozen subspecies of this geographically variable sparrow have been recognized, but research indicates that all are genetically similar.

Date and Location Seen: _____

Description: 5.75″. Skulking sparrow of dense, wet, shrubby areas. **Breast is washed with buff** and is **finely-streaked** (usually a small central breast spot). Also has broad, gray eyebrow, narrow buff eye-ring, and **buffy whisker mark**. Wings are tinged rusty. Slender and long-tailed, with **peaked crown**.

Similar Species: Song Sparrow (p. 367) is more boldly streaked and lacks buffy breast.

Voice: Call is low *thik*. Song is hurried warble, usually rising and then falling in pitch.

Where to Find: Fairly common to uncommon migrant (April-May, September-October) and fairly common summer resident of mid- to high-elevation wet meadows, bogs, and thickets. Visits lowland brushy areas during migration. Rare in winter.

Behavior: Forages on the ground under cover for insects and seeds. Moves furtively through low, dense weedy growth and damp brushy areas. In migration, seldom forms pure flocks, but joins other migrating or resident sparrows.

Did you Know? This sparrow was named by Audubon in 1833, not for Honest Abe but for Thomas Lincoln.

Date and Location Seen: _____

_____

White-throated Sparrow

White-crowned Sparrow
Adult

White-crowned Sparrow
Immature

Description: 7"/6.75". Fairly large, long-tailed sparrows with unstreaked gray breasts and grayish-brown upperparts. WHITE-CROWNED: Has **bold black and white crown stripes**; gray underparts; streaked back; orange-pink, yellow, or dark pink bill. In immatures, crown stripes are dark brown and gray with buff crown center. WHITE-THROATED: Similar to White-crown, but with **clearly-marked white throat**, rusty-brown upperparts, and **bright yellow spot in front of eye**.

Similar Species: Golden-crowned Sparrow (p. 373) has golden-yellow crown bordered by black, and a darker bill.

Voice: WHITE-CROWNED: Call is sharp *pink*, lower and drier than metallic *chink* of White-throated; song consists of clear whistles followed by buzzes and trills. WHITE-THROATED: Song is diagnostic *see see serr prididit prididit prididit*.

Where to Find: WHITE-CROWNED: Common migrant (April-May, August-November) and uncommon and local summer resident of mid- to high-elevation brushy meadows and dense shrub lands. Uncommon to fairly common in winter, mainly in the Columbia and Klamath Basins and Snake River Valley. Rare elsewhere. WHITE-THROATED: Rare migrant and winter resident, usually with White-crowned and Golden-crowned Sparrows.

Behavior: Both species forage on the ground for insects, seeds, and fruit in brushy areas, and fly into dense cover when flushed. They readily visit backyard feeders.

Did you Know? Unlike many songbirds, both species often sing at night on their breeding grounds.

Date and Location Seen: _____

Golden-crowned Sparrow
Breeding Adult

Golden-crowned Sparrow
Immature

Harris's Sparrow
Breeding

Harris's Sparrow
Non-breeding

Description: 7.25"/7.5". **Large** sparrows. GOLDEN-CROWNED: **Dull gray below**, with streaked brownish back, dull pinkish-gray bill, and a **yellow patch on the forecrown**. Adult's crown is bordered with black; forehead is bright yellow (pattern bolder in breeding plumage, with black extending down to eyes). Immature's head is plainer, with dull yellow tinge to forehead. HARRIS'S: Adult has **black crown and throat**, gray (breeding) or buff (non-breeding) face, **white underparts with dark-streaked flanks**, streaked brownish back, **pink bill**, gray (adult) or buff face. Immature is like non-breeding adult, except crown is brownish and throat is white with dark brown necklace.

Similar Species: Smaller immature White-crowned Sparrow (p. 371) lacks yellow on crown.

Voice: GOLDEN-CROWNED: Call is slurred *chink*. HARRIS'S: Call is loud *chip*.

Where to Find: GOLDEN-CROWNED: Fairly common migrant (September-October, April-May) and uncommon winter resident of lowland riparian woodlands and thickets on east slopes of Cascade Mountains in central Oregon and Washington. Rare elsewhere. HARRIS'S: Rare migrant and winter resident.

Behavior: GOLDEN-CROWNED: Makes short distance migrations from Cascade Mountains to nearby lowlands in fall. HARRIS'S: Migrates mainly east of the Rocky Mountains. Joins winter foraging flocks of similar-size sparrows.

Did you Know? These beautiful sparrows are rare in most of our region. Birders usually discover them among White-crowned Sparrow flocks, often at feeders.

Date and Location Seen: _____

_____

Oregon Male

Oregon Female

Slate-colored

Oregon Juvenile

Description: 6″. **Dark-hooded sparrows** with **light pink bill** and **flashing white outer tail feathers**. Three distinct forms in region. "Oregon" male has **black head** contrasting with **pinkish-brown back**, white chest, and **pinkish sides**. Female's head color ranges from slate-gray to pale gray. "Slate-colored" birds have slaty or gray-brown backs and slate gray sides (paler and washed with brown in females). "Pink-sided" birds are similar to "Oregon" types, but with blue-gray hoods, black lores, pale gray throat, pinkish flanks, and brown back. Juveniles are streaked above and below.

Similar Species: Immature juncos similar to Vesper Sparrow (p. 357), but lack the sparrow's facial pattern and have pink bills.

Voice: Call is high, hard *stip*; song is simple, musical trill.

Where to Find: Common summer forest residents of mid- to high-elevations, also common migrants and winter residents (September-May) of low-elevation valleys.

Behavior: Forages on the ground for insects and seeds. Nests are constructed almost always on the ground on a sloping bank or rock face, often hidden in depressions, under grasses, or other cover. Commonly makes fall altitudinal migrations to lower elevations.

Did you Know? The "Slate-colored" form breeds in Canada and Alaska, but migrates through and winters in our region. Until 1973, it and the other junco forms were considered separate species.

Date and Location Seen: _____

_____

Snow Bunting
Winter

Lapland Longspur

SNOW BUNTING/LAPLAND LONGSPUR
Plectrophenax nivalis / Calcarius lapponicus

Description: 6.75"/6.25". Small Arctic finches that winter in open fields. All have tiny conical bills. BUNTING: Breeding male is **white overall** with **black back**, and **black and white wings and tail**. Breeding female like male, but with grayish head and rufous streaking on back. Non-breeding and immature birds have white underparts with rusty breast band, rusty head and flanks, mottled rust and black back. LAPLAND: All plumages have **mottled rust and brown upperparts**, streaked flanks, white belly, and **brown tail with white outer feathers**. Breeding male has black head with white frame, black breast, rufous nape, and black flank streaks. Females and immatures have rusty heads with dark ear patch, and diffuse breast band.

Similar Species: Horned Lark (p. 261) has solid brown back and wings; long, mostly black tail.

Voice: SNOW: Call is clear, descending *cheew*, and a soft, husky rattle. LAPLAND: Call is husky *teeew* and dry rattle *trididit*.

Where to Find: Uncommon-rare migrants and winter residents (November-March) of open valleys. Most regular in Montana and eastern Idaho. Both species are irruptive, with unpredictable winter presence.

Behavior: Both species forage on ground for seeds in plowed or sparsely vegetated fields. Flocks wander widely.

Did you Know? These species often form large flocks with Horned Larks, and feed on open, wind-swept crop fields in winter.

Date and Location Seen: _____

Male

Female

Description: 8.25". **Very thick, conical bi-colored bill**; **white wing patterning and yellow underwing linings** are distinctive in all plumages. ADULT: **Male's head** is **mostly black**; back streaked; **collar, breast, sides, and rump rich orange**; black wings and tail have bold white markings. IMMATURE: Male is duller, with striped head. Female has **brown crown stripes** and eye-line; **tawny, streaked breast**; brown wings with few white markings.

Similar Species: American Robin (p. 311) lacks white in the wings. Very similar female Rose-breasted Grosbeak (rare) has distinctly streaked whitish breast.

Voice: Call is sharp *pik*; song is rollicking and varied series of rich, whistled notes.

Where to Find: Common migrant (May-June, August-September) and summer resident throughout the region in riparian woodlands, open mixed forests, cottonwood thickets, and aspen groves.

Behavior: Arboreal forager, takes fruits, berries, seeds, and insects. Male and female both sing, sometimes even from the nest or in flight.

Did you Know? Male Black-headed Grosbeaks stop singing in July, and then disperse. The females and young remain for several weeks longer before migrating.

Date and Location Seen: _____

_____

Breeding Adult
Male

Female

Description: 5.5". A finch-like bird with **wing-bars**. MALE: **Head and upperparts are bright blue, breast is tawny-orange**, belly and wing-bars are white. IMMATURE MALES: More limited blue. FEMALE: Has **plain** gray-brown head and upperparts, **tawny breast, narrow white to buffy wing-bars**. JUVENILE: Resembles female, but breast is finely streaked.

Similar Species: Western Bluebird (p. 301) has rusty-brown back, lacks finch-like bill and wing-bars. Indigo Bunting (rare) lacks wing-bars and white belly.

Voice: Call is sharp *pit*; song is rapid, jumbled warble, with many notes given in pairs.

Where to Find: Common migrant and summer resident (May-September) of brushy areas. Found in dense riparian thickets and shrubby areas of uplands.

Behavior: Diet is mainly insects and seeds. When foraging, gleans food from foliage, hops along the ground, or flies out to catch aerial prey. Builds nest low in thick shrubs or small trees. Does not nest in sagebrush. Female chooses the nest site and builds the nest.

Did you Know? No two male Lazuli Buntings have breeding songs that sound exactly alike.

Date and Location Seen: _____

Male

Female

Description: 7". Distinctive medium-size meadow dwelling song-bird with a short, conical bill. BREEDING MALE: **Black head, wings, tail, and underparts; prominent straw-colored nape; broad white shoulder patch and white rump.** FEMALE and NON-BREEDING MALE: Underparts yellowish buff, upperparts brown with black streaks on back, flanks, and undertail; wings and tail brown; head is buff with dark stripes through eye and on crown.

Similar Species: Grasshopper Sparrow (rare) resembles female Bobolink but is smaller with a larger head and shorter tail.

Voice: Call is low *chuk*; song is long, bubbly series of warbling notes.

Where to Find: Rare to fairly common summer resident (May-September) of wet meadows. Seen near P Ranch in Malheur N.W.R, Oregon; along Toppenish Creek and Calispell Lake, Washington; Grays Lake N.W.R., Idaho; and along Bass Creek, Montana.

Behavior: Forages for seeds and insects on the ground or while perched on vegetation. Males are conspicuous, either singing from exposed perches or while making display flights over meadows. Nests colonially in widely scattered locations. Males molt out of bright plumage in late summer and then resemble females and immatures

Did you Know? Bobolinks are extraordinary long-distance migrants, traveling thousands of miles from their breeding areas in Canada to wintering areas in South America.

Date and Location Seen: _____

_____

Red-winged Blackbird Male

Red-winged Blackbird Female

Tri-colored Blackbird Male

Tri-colored Blackbird Female

Description: 8.75". RED-WINGED: Familiar dark-eyed black-bird of wetlands. Male is **black** overall, with **bright red shoulder patch** bordered behind by creamy yellow. Female is dark brown, heavily streaked above and below, with buffy eyebrow and throat, reddish-brown tint to wings and back. TRICOLORED: Male is similar to Red-winged, but has **deep red shoulder patch bordered by broad white stripe**. Female is **sooty gray** with **whitish streaking on breast**, pale eyebrow.

Similar Species: Brewer's Blackbird (p. 391) has pale yellow eyes and lacks shoulder patches, female is unstreaked.

Voice: RED-WINGED: Call is sharp *chek*; song is musical *cong-ka-REEE*. TRICOLORED: Compared to Red-winged's, call is lower-pitched and song is harsh and nasal.

Where to Find: RED-WINGED: Common resident of marshes and riparian areas. TRICOLORED: Common resident of Klamath Basin, near Prineville, Oregon, and Othello, Washington. Locally common summer resident (March-July) and rare in winter in scattered wetlands in Oregon and Washington. Increasing in the region.

Behavior: Both forage for seeds, insects. They travel widely to feed in fields and grasslands. Nest colonially in marshes with tall emergent vegetation, usually with cattails and bulrushes.

Did you Know? When male Red-winged and Tricolored Black-birds are not displaying, their large, colorful shoulder patches are often completely covered by other feathers, leaving only the yellow or white edges visible.

Date and Location Seen: _____

_____

385

Description: 9.5". **Stocky and short-tailed** bird of open areas with a long, pointed bill. Cryptic gray-brown above; head has bold stripes. **Bright yellow below with black "V" on breast** and streaked white sides. Tail is bordered with white. Winter birds and immatures are less boldly marked.

Similar Species: Distinctive.

Voice: Call is harsh *chuck*; song is bubbly burst of fluty whistles.

Where to Find: Common migrant (March-April, August-September) and summer resident of meadows, pastures, and rangeland. Uncommon to rare and local in winter. Regularly winters in lower Columbia Basin and other open, low-elevation areas.

Behavior: Seen in pairs or small groups in open country, foraging for insects and seeds. Walks on ground, flicking open white-edged tail. Males sing from atop shrubs, boulders, fence posts, or other high perches. After the breeding season, large flocks form to feed together through winter.

Did you Know? Western Meadowlark is nearly identical to Eastern Meadowlark, but the two species have very different songs.

Date and Location Seen: _____

_____

Male

Female

Description: 6.25"/6.5". RED: Stocky coniferous forest finch with relatively large head, **heavy bill with crossed tips, dark wings**, dark notched tail. Typical **adult male** is **brick-red, female** is **dull olive**, and juvenile is grayish-brown and heavily streaked. WHITE-WINGED: Medium-size boreal forest finch that has **dark wings with bold white wing-bars, slender bill with crossed tips**, and dark notched tail. **Adult male** is **pinkish-red**, flanks grayish. **Female** is **olive-gray**, indistinctly streaked on flanks. Juvenile is brown and heavily streaked. Immature males of both species duller.

Similar Species: Larger Pine Grosbeak (p. 399) lacks crossed bill tips. Pine Siskin (p. 407) lacks bold wing-bars and crossed bill tips.

Voice: RED: Flight call is *kip-kip-kip*; song is variable series of short notes, warbles. WHITE-WINGED: Call is *chut-chut-chut*; song is series of rattling trills.

Where to Find: RED: Common, but nomadic resident of mature coniferous forests. WHITE-WINGED: Uncommon to rare, nomadic visitor to mature coniferous forests.

Behavior: Both species form foraging flocks. Usually feed in tall conifer trees, prying open cones for seed. Both also feed on other seeds, buds, insects, and minerals from soil. Opportunistic wandering breeders, they nest wherever and whenever they find sufficiently large cone seed crops, even during winter.

Did you Know? The distinctive crossed bill tips of crossbills are well-adapted tools for extracting seeds from cones.

Date and Location Seen: _____

_____

Brewer's Blackbird
Male

Brewer's Blackbird
Female

Common Grackle
Male

Common Grackle
Female

Description: 9"/12.5". BREWER'S: Common, conspicuous black-bird with fairly short, pointed bill and medium-long tail. Male is **shiny black** throughout, with iridescent green and purple highlights; **pale yellow eyes**. Female is **solidly dull gray-brown** with dark eyes. GRACKLE: **Larger, heavier, with longer, thicker bill**; **shiny black** throughout. Male is deep, iridescent purplish-blue on head, neck, and breast, otherwise brassy bronze. **Tail is long, keeled** in flight. Eyes are yellow. Female and immature smaller, duller.

Similar Species: Smaller Brown-headed Cowbird (p. 393) has smaller, thicker bill, shorter tail. Immature European Starling (p. 319) has longer bill, shorter tail.

Voice: BREWER'S: Call is high, sharp *check*; song is high *k-squeesh*. GRACKLE: Call is harsh *chack*; song is unmusical *readle-eak*.

Where to Find: BREWER'S: Common migrant (March-May, September-November) and summer resident of open agricultural areas, residential neighborhoods, and grasslands. Uncommon in winter; usually in lowland agricultural areas. GRACKLE: Uncommon to rare and local breeder in western Montana and southern Idaho. Rare migrant elsewhere.

Behavior: Both forage on the ground in small flocks mainly for insects and seeds, often in residential areas. Males deliver songs while fluffing plumage and spreading tail. Nest in colonies in dense shrubs or trees, often small conifers. Although colonial nesters, they aggressively defend territories.

Did you Know? Common Grackles are rapidly expanding their range into the West.

Date and Location Seen: _____

Male

Female

Juvenile

Description: 7.5″. **Small, short-tailed blackbird** with **dark eyes** and a **stubby, finch-like bill**. MALE: Black throughout, with a **dark brown head**. FEMALE: Plain gray-brown.

Similar Species: Brewer's Blackbird (p. 391) has thinner bill, longer tail; male has pale eyes and shiny black head, female sootier.

Voice: Calls include sharp rattle and high flight whistles; song is gurgling *glug-glug-gleeee*, delivered with bowed head and partially spread wings and tail.

Where to Find: Common migrant (April-May, July-September) and summer resident of riparian woodlands and other open areas with scattered trees. Frequents agricultural areas, but avoids dense coniferous forests. After breeding season, joins mixed blackbird species migratory flocks. Rare in winter, occasionally persists among mixed blackbird flocks at livestock feedlots.

Behavior: Forages mainly on the ground for seeds and insects. Breeding males display and chase females. As brood parasites, females lay eggs in the nests of other songbirds which then raise the cowbird fledglings. Highly gregarious in all seasons.

Did you Know? Increasing populations of cowbirds, along with modern agriculture, fragmentation of forest habitats, and urbanization have negatively impacted many species of songbirds. Intensive, targeted cowbird trapping has aided some of the most threatened host species.

Date and Location Seen: _____

_____

Male

Immature Male

Female

Description: 9". Medium-size slender bird with long tail, dark and tapered sharp bill. ADULT MALE: **Bright orange** or yellow-orange on underparts, rump and face. **Black crown**, eye-line, and stripe on chin. **Large white patches on wings. Tail** is **orange-yellow with black center and tip**. FEMALE: Has gray back, pale grayish-white belly. Head and breast are yellow-orange. Rump and tail are dull yellowish. IMMATURE MALE: Resembles female, but with black chin and eye-line.

Similar Species: Male Black-headed Grosbeak (p. 379) has very thick bill and different plumage pattern. Female Western Tanager (p. 347) has smaller, thicker, orangish bill.

Voice: Call is harsh *scheek*; song is rollicking *chik-chicky-tew-tew*.

Where to Find: Common migrant (April-May, August-September) and summer resident of lowland and foothill riparian woodlands and residential deciduous groves.

Behavior: Forages for insects and fruit within the foliage of broad-leafed trees, especially cottonwoods and willows. Builds sturdy, pendulous basket-shaped nests that hang from small deciduous tree branches. Male loudly and aggressively defends territory and usually departs from nesting area long before female and young

Did you Know? Orioles occasionally construct their nests with green plastic Easter basket "grass", monofilament fishing line, or bailing twine.

Date and Location Seen: _____

_____

Gray-crowned Rosy-Finch

Gray-crowned Rosy-Finch
Interior Race

Black Rosy-Finch

Description: 6.25″. GRAY-CROWNED: A **cinnamon-brown** ground finch with a **gray head**, yellow bill (winter), **black forehead and throat. Belly, rump, and wings are washed with pink**. Females paler. BLACK: **Blackish with gray across the back of head**, yellow bill (winter), **pink wash on belly, rump, and wings**. Females are paler.

Similar Species: Similar finches lack gray on their heads.

Voice: Both species give a soft, low *cheew*.

Where to Find: Summer residents of alpine areas on mountain tops. Flocks move to lower elevations in winter. Both are uncommon to rare and local summer residents, rare winter residents in foothills and valleys. GRAY-CROWNED: Widespread in the region. In summer, often seen at Logan Pass in Glacier National Park, Montana. BLACK: Breeds locally southward from central Idaho and western Montana; also at Steens Mountain, Oregon. May occasionally breed in Wallowa Mountains of Oregon. Both species winter in Sun Valley, Idaho.

Behavior: Diet is mostly insects and seeds gleaned from bare ground or snow, especially at snowline.

Did you Know? In winter, both species are highly gregarious and often found together. They form large, communal evening roosts in abandoned Cliff Swallow nests, caves, mine shafts, barns, and cavities on cliff faces.

Date and Location Seen: _____

_____

Male

Female

Description: 9". Large, round-headed boreal finch with dark gray wings and **two bold white wing-bars. Tail is long, bill is short** and **rounded**. MALE: Has **rose-colored upperparts**; underparts are variably gray and rose. FEMALE: Gray overall with a variable wash of olive on head and upperparts.

Similar Species: Smaller White-winged Crossbill (p. 405) has a longer, crossed bill.

Voice: Call is musical *teew teew teew*; song is clear, distinct finch-type warble.

Where to Find: Uncommon and local summer resident of mid- to high-elevation forests in the Rockies, Blue, and Wallowa Mountains, and the Washington Cascades and Okanogan Highlands. Rare in winter (November-March) in lowland areas. Wintering numbers unpredictable from year to year.

Behavior: Forages on the ground, in trees, shrubs, and in the air. Diet is mainly buds, seeds, fruits, berries, and some insects. In winter they are typically seen in small flocks. Occasionally makes short, downslope migrations in winter.

Did you Know? Pine Grosbeaks are renowned for their quietness, slow movements, and apparent lack of fear of humans. Many feeding flocks likely go unnoticed by birders because they seldom flush or become agitated when approached by people.

Date and Location Seen: _____

_____

Cassin's Finch
Male

Cassin's Finch
Female

Purple Finch
Adult Male

Purple Finch
Female

CASSIN'S FINCH/PURPLE FINCH

Carpodacus cassinii / Carpodacus purpureus

Description: 6.25"/6". Mountain finches with stout bills and **notched tails**. CASSIN'S: Adult male has **red crown**, pink-washed face, throat, breast and rump; fine streaks on flanks; distinct **back streaks**. Wings and tail brownish, belly white. Female is grayish-brown with fine black streaks above, **short, crisp brownish streaks** on white below; head brown with indistinct whitish eyebrow and cheek patch; thin, pale eye-ring. PURPLE: Adult male has **raspberry-red head, breast and rump**. Brown back and wings pinkish; blurry streaks on sides. Female's **patterned head** has dark ear patch and crown, indistinct whitish eyebrow and whisker stripe; **blurry brown stripes below**; olive-brown back with blurry streaks.

Similar Species: Male House Finch (p. 403) has smaller bill and head, longer tail, and more extensive streaking on belly and flanks;

Voice: CASSIN'S: Call is musical *tr-dlip*. PURPLE: Call is sharp *pik* or *whee-oo*. Songs of both are rapid warbles; Cassin's is higher and brighter.

Where to Find: CASSIN'S: Common resident of open, dry coniferous forests. PURPLE: Uncommon to rare resident of moist forest habitats and residential areas.

Behavior: Both forage for seeds, buds, and some insects. Form small flocks in the fall and make seasonal movements tied to food availability.

Did you Know? Both finches are accomplished mimics, often incorporating the songs of other birds into their musical repertoire.

Date and Location Seen: _____

_____

Male

Female

Description: 6". Common and familiar songbird with a **short, rounded bill** and long, slightly notched tail. MALE: Variably **red to orange-red** on crown, throat, breast, and rump; **sides and belly have long, distinct streaks**. FEMALE: Gray-brown overall, with **long gray-brown blurry streaks below. Head is relatively plain and unpatterned**.

Similar Species: Male Cassin's and Purple Finches (p. 401) lack distinct streaks on underparts, have larger heads and shorter tails; females have strong facial patterns.

Voice: Calls include variety of bright, inflected *chirp* notes. Song is cheery, musical warble, descending slightly and ending with a long, burry note.

Where to Find: Primarily an urban species. Common resident of low-elevation residential areas, farmlands, and pastures.

Behavior: Abundant and unwary, often nesting in planters, on porches, and under eaves. Feeds on seeds and buds; commonly visits seed feeders. Often forms flocks in non-breeding season.

Did you Know? The red coloration of male House Finches is derived from pigments called carotenoids in the foods they eat. The more pigment the male ingests, the redder he becomes. Female House Finches preferentially select the reddest males available as breeding partners, perhaps because these males are seemingly the healthiest and would be expected to be the best providers for her and her brood.

Date and Location Seen: _____

Red Crossbill Male

Red Crossbill Female

White-Winged Crossbill Male

White-Winged Crossbill Female

Description: 9.5″ (male), 8.5″ (female). Large and distinctive marsh blackbird. MALE: **Black body** contrasts with **bright yellow head, neck and breast**; has large **white wing patch**; vent area is yellow. FEMALE: Dark brown with dingy yellow on face, neck, and breast; vent area is yellow. IMMATURE: Faded version of adult male or female.

Similar Species: All other blackbirds lack yellow in plumage.

Voice: Call is low, rich *k-ruk*; song is harsh, unmusical.

Where to Find: Common migrant (April-May, July-September) and summer resident of cattails and bulrush marshes. Rare and local in winter.

Behavior: Forages on aquatic insects, grains, and seeds. Although territorial around nest site, often joins large multi-species blackbird flocks feeding in pastures or farm fields near the nesting area. Male displays by singing from elevated perches, spreading wings and tail, and holding bill pointed upward. Nests colonially in marsh vegetation, always over water. Nomadic after breeding season; flocks forage widely over agricultural fields, meadows, and other open areas. Roosts nightly with other blackbirds in marshes.

Did you Know? Yellow-headed Blackbirds often nest near Red-winged Blackbirds in marshes, but usually occupy the portions of the marsh with deeper water and emergent vegetation.

Date and Location Seen: _____

_____

Pine Siskin

Common Redpoll

Description: 5"/5.25". SISKIN: **Small** brown bird with short, **notched tail**, long wings, and **thin, pointed bill**. **Streaked above and below**, with **yellow fringes on wings**. Brightest birds have **broad yellow wing-bars, yellow stripe on spread wing**, and yellow wash on breast. REDPOLL: **Small**, streaked brownish above, **white below** with coarse black streaking on flanks. **Forehead is red, bill base and throat are black**. Male has **rose-pink breast**.

Similar Species: Larger female House Finch (p. 403) has short, thick bill and lacks yellow plumage. Hoary Redpoll (rare) is very similar to Common Redpoll, but larger, paler; has smaller bill, white rump and undertail.

Voice: SISKIN: Calls include *sheee-u* and buzzy, rising *zzhreeee*; song is mix of calls and trills. REDPOLL: Call is *chit chit chit*; song is series of trilling, buzzy notes.

Where to Find: SISKIN: Common, but irruptive resident of coniferous forests. After breeding, disperses widely. REDPOLL: Uncommon to rare winter resident (November-March) of open, brushy areas and riparian woodlands. Irruptive and unpredictable, most regular from Oregon's Blue Mountains and central Idaho northward.

Behavior: Diet of both is mainly seeds and insects; also readily use bird feeders. Both form post-breeding season flocks. Irregular visitors to lowland valleys, depending upon food availability.

Did you Know? Pine Siskin is the most frequent "winter finch" to visit backyard bird feeders.

Date and Location Seen: _____

_____

**American Goldfinch
Breeding Male**

**American Goldfinch
Female**

**Lesser Goldfinch
Male**

**Lesser Goldfinch
Female**

Description: 5"/4.5". AMERICAN: All plumages have black wings and tail, **prominent wing-bars**, white undertail, **conical bill** (pink in summer). BREEDING: Male: **Bright-yellow** with black forehead. Female: Olive above, yellow below. NON-BREEDING: Tan above, gray below, yellow on throat and "shoulder" of male. LESSER: Male is **olive-green above, bright-yellow below**; crown black. Black **wings and tail have large white wing patches**. Female is like male, but duller; lacks black crown, reduced white in wings.

Similar Species: Female Lazuli Bunting (p. 381) lacks white patches on wings and tail.

Voice: AMERICAN: Flight call is *yip-yip*; song is high, musical series. LESSER: Call is high *tee-yee* or *tee-yur*; song is collection of call notes.

Where to Find: AMERICAN: Common resident of riparian woodlands, residential areas, and farmland. LESSER: Uncommon and local resident in open, dry areas. Regular in Klickitat County, Washington and southern portions of Oregon and Idaho. Rare elsewhere.

Behavior: Both forage for seeds and visit backyard feeders, breed in loose colonial groups, and defending territories near nests. After breeding, they congregate in nomadic flocks.

Did you Know? American Goldfinches are very late nesters, delaying their breeding until after thistles have produced seed. Thistles provide an important food source for this species as well as material for lining their nests.

Date and Location Seen: _____

_____

Male

Female

Description: 8″. Stocky, short-tailed finch with a **massive head and conical pale greenish-yellow bill**, black wings with **large white wing patches**, and a black tail. MALE: Dark brownish head with **bold yellow eyebrow**; dark brown head and breast fade to yellow on the back and belly. FEMALE: Brownish gray above, gray below.

Similar Species: Black-headed Grosbeak (p. 379) lacks the yellow eyebrow of the Evening male and the unpatterned head of the female. Much smaller American Goldfinch (p. 409) has a small bill.

Voice: Calls include high, bell-like *kleer* and high whistled *teew* notes in flight.

Where to Find: Fairly common, summer resident of mid- to high-elevation coniferous forests. Moves downslope in fall and winters in lower elevation forests, riparian woodlands, and residential areas. Somewhat nomadic, may leave the region in years of poor food supplies.

Behavior: Wanders widely; forages for a variety of seeds, buds, fruits, and insects. Typically feeds at the tops and outer branches of trees. Large numbers gather in forests infested by spruce budworm. Regularly visits bird feeders.

Did you Know? Evening Grosbeak's bill is very powerful and can crack even the very hardest of seeds.

Date and Location Seen: _____

_____

Male

Female

Description: 6.25″. Chunky, familiar, introduced sparrow with a stout bill. MALE: Has **black bib** (somewhat obscured by gray feather tips in fall, winter), **gray crown**, pale gray cheeks, **rufous neck sides** and rufous areas on striped back and wings; prominent, white wing-bars. Bill is black in breeding season, otherwise yellowish. FEMALE: Dingy gray-brown with tan and brown back stripes; has broad, creamy eyebrow and dull yellowish bill.

Similar Species: Our native sparrows are slimmer, have shorter and more sharply-pointed bills, and differ in face pattern.

Voice: Calls are frequent *chirp* or *cheep* notes; song is monotonous series of call notes.

Where to Find: Common resident of human-modified areas, usually agricultural and residential areas.

Behavior: Picks seeds, grains, crumbs, or insects from the ground. Forms small nesting colonies. Nest is a ball of dried vegetation mixed with feathers and other detritus placed in cavities or crevices of trees, structures, or buildings. Flocks regularly visit bird feeders.

Did you Know? House Sparrows were first introduced to the U.S. in 1850, but did not reach some portions of our region for another 50 years or so.

Date and Location Seen: _____

_____

Acknowledgments, Photographer Credits

Thanks to Harry Nehls who initially suggested this book and wrote the first draft of the species account text. Some of the book's text has been modeled after *Birds of the Los Angeles Region* and we appreciate authors Jon Dunn's and Kimball Garrett's permission to use their text in this manner. Dave Trochlell, Regional Editor for Idaho and Western Montana for *North American Birds*, wrote the final draft of the species accounts and together with his wife Cathy did a masterful job of editing the book. Mike Denny suggested a number of regional photographers who provided the quality bird images in this book. Thanks to Gina Calle for the design and layout of the book, Shawn K. Morse for the Inland Northwest and Northern Rockies map, Eric Kraig for the bird drawings, and Christina Morse for her tireless support and suggestions.

We owe a great debt to the many photographers who have contributed to this book, consistently meeting the challenge of capturing a bird's key field marks in photographs of high technical and artistic merit. Their names are listed below. In particular, Herb Clarke, Tom Munson, Laure Wilson Neish, Brian Small, Khanh Tran, George Vlahakis, Michael Woodruff, and Tim Zurowski, spent hours searching for just the right images for us. Special thanks to Peter Stahl for permission to use his Osprey photo on the front cover and Khanh Tran for the use of his Wood Duck photo on the back cover.

The letters following the page numbers refer to the position of the photograph on that page (T = top, B = bottom, L = left, R = right, N = inset).

Don Baccus: 82T. **Lee Barnes:** 32BL, 50B, 60, 96, 118T, B, 130TL, 164T, 170, 176, 190B, 218TL, 270, 328T. **Tony Beck/VIREO:** 196N. **Rick and Nora Bowers:** 42T, 76B, 102BL, 144R, 166R, 242B. **Keith Brady:** 20T, 94, 126T, 152TR, 174, 252, 262B, 276B, 392BL, 400BL, BR, 410T, B. **Jim Burns:** 152BL. **Steve Cannings:** 310B, 346B. **A. & S. Carey/VIREO:** 56B. **Herb Clarke:** 20B, BN, 132TN, 138BL, 148BR, 348TL, 408TL. **Richard Day/VIREO:** 400TL. **Mike Donahue:** 112TN, 154BL, BR, 158T. **Mike Dossett:** 28B, 62T, 64TL, 66T, 168T, 244, 316. **Tom Eckert:** 58T, B, 278TL, 334T, B. **James R. Gallagher/Sea & Sand Audubon:** 404TL. **Don Graham:** 48TR. **Denny Granstrand:** 188, 192, 348BL, BR, 398T. **Carrie Griffis:** 404TR. **Joe Higbee:** 78, 152TL, 228. **Ralph Hocken:** 36T, 52TR, BL, BR, 134T, 164B,

224B, 290B, 312T, B, 384TL. **Julian Hough:** 114BR, 154TR, 156B, 246T, 398B. **Jerry Liguori:** 116BL, BR, 162BL, 302. **Dan Logen:** 214TL, TR, 300TL, TR. **Gary Luhm:** 126B. **Stuart MacKay:** 124T, 144TR, 148T, 150T. **Dick McNeely:** 72B, 102BR, 108B, 112T, 194B, 236T, 238B, 256, 320, 372TR. **Tom Munson:** 90T, 114TL, 182, 232. **Laure Wilson Neish:** 46B, 274T, 370B, 406B. **Dennis Paulson:** 192TN, 256TN. **Jim Pruske:** 18TN, 48TL, BL, BR, 84, 120, 178, 196, 220T, B, 248, 280, 318BN, 322TR, 372TL, 374BR, 378T, B, 384TR, 390TR, 392T, BR, 412T. **Jim Robertson:** 24B. **Mike Roper:** 106B, 268. **Jim Rosso:** 272TN. **Robert Royse:** 18, 32TL, TR, 34B, 44B, TN, 54T, B, 130BL, 134B, 138TR, 140T, 152BR, 162BR, 190T, 200BR, 204B, 288B, 300BR, 352T, 370TN, 374BL, 386. **Bart Rulon:** 24T, 30BR, 68T, 74BL, 88B, 128BL, 136, 138BR, 146, 374TL, 402T, B. **Larry Sansone:** 22B, 28TN, 34TN, 44T, 78TN, 82TN, 90B, 98BR, 102TR, 116TL, 128TR, 132, 140B, 142B, 162TL, 194BN, 198, 200TR, 202B, 212B, 224T, 240T, 260B, 262TN, 264TN, 270TN, 278BR, 330BL, 354, 358, 360B, 364, 366, 368, 370T, 384BR, 388T, 390TL, BL, 408TR. **Michael Shepard, www.birdinfo. com:** 22T, 154TL, 156T, 158B, 258TN. **Brian Small:** 28T, 32BR, 38B, 40T, B, TN, 42B, 62BL, BR, 64BL, 66B, 68B, TN, 70TN, 74TL, TR, BR, 76T, 80, 82B, 88T, 92, 94TN, 96TN, 102TL, 110, 114TR, 128TL, BR, 130TR, BR, 142T, 144TL, 150B, 160, 162TR, 168B, 172, 194T, 200TL, 202T, 204TN, 208, 210T, B, 214BR, 218TR, 226T, B, 230T, B, 234, 236B, 238T, 240B, 242T, 260T, 266, 272, 274B, 278TR, BL, 284, 288T, 290T, 296, 304, 306, 308, 310T, 314, 318T, 322BL, 324, 326T, B, 328B, 330TL, TR, BR, 332T, B, 336T, B, 338, 340B, 342T, B, 344, 346T, 352B, 356, 362T, B, 372BL, 374TR, 380B, 384BL, 388B, 390BR, 394B, BN, 396B, 406T, 408BL, BR, 412B. **Margaret St. Clair:** 38T, 50T, 52TL, 70T, 72T, 214BL, 262T, 292. **Peter Stahl:** front cover. **Ruth Sullivan:** 200BL. **Khanh Tran:** 26T, 64TR, BR, 380T, back cover. **Hank Tseng:** 26B, 30TL, BL, 46T, 70B, 98TR, 100T, B, 124B, 148BL, 206T, 258, 276B, 298B, 300BL, 322TL. **Idie Ulsh:** 166T. **George Vlahakis:** 100TN, 184, 186, 212T, 216T, B, 218BL, BR, 222, 250, 360T, 372BR. **Barry Wahl:** 30TR, 86, 264, 294, 298T, 318B, 340T. **Brian Wheeler:** 20TN, 98TL, BL, 104T, B, 106T, 108T, 112B, 122. **John Williams:** 34T. **Cathy Wise:** 394T. **Michael Woodruff:** 56T, 114BL, 180, 286, 382B, 396TR. **Jim Zipp:** 116TR, 206B, 246B, 254, 322BR, 350, 382T, 396TL, 404BL, BR. **William Zittrich:** 204T. **Tim Zurowski:** 36B, 40BN, 44BN, 138TL, 282, 376T, B, 400TR.

The success of this guide is the success of all those who contributed to it. Their participation is sincerely appreciated.

Index/Checklist of Birds of the Inland Northwest and Northern Rockies

Use this checklist to keep a record of the birds you have seen. Bold numbers are for the main Species Account page. Birds shown in the Common Local Birds section of the book are denoted by 'clb".

- ☐ Avocet, American, **129**
- ☐ Bittern, American, **85**
- ☐ Blackbird, Brewer's, clb, 385, 319, **391**, 393
- ☐ Red-winged, clb, 383, **385**
- ☐ Tri-colored, **385**
- ☐ Yellow-headed, **389**
- ☐ Bluebird, Mountain, **301**, 303
- ☐ Western, **301**, 381
- ☐ Bobolink, **383**
- ☐ Bufflehead, **47**, 49, 51, 55
- ☐ Bunting, Lazuli, 301, **381**
- ☐ Snow, **377**
- ☐ Bushtit, **279**
- ☐ Canvasback, **41**
- ☐ Catbird, Gray, **315**
- ☐ Chat, Yellow-breasted, **345**
- ☐ Chickadee, Black-capped, clb, **275**, 277
- ☐ Chestnut-backed, **277**
- ☐ Mountain, clb, 275, **277**
- ☐ Chukar, **57**
- ☐ Coot, American, clb, **121**
- ☐ Cormorant, Double-crested, **83**
- ☐ Cowbird, Brown-headed, 391, **393**

- ☐ Crane, Sandhill, 87, **123**
- ☐ Creeper, Brown, **287**
- ☐ Crossbill, Red, **405**
- ☐ White-winged, 399, **405**
- ☐ Crow, American, clb, **257**, 259
- ☐ Curlew, Long-billed, **137**, 145
- ☐ Dipper, American, **297**
- ☐ Dove, Eurasian Collared-, **169**
- ☐ Mourning, clb, **169**
- ☐ Dowitcher, Long-billed, **145**, 147
- ☐ Duck, Ring-necked, 41, **43**, 45
- ☐ Ruddy, **55**
- ☐ Wood, **27**
- ☐ Dunlin, **143**
- ☐ Eagle, Bald, 97, **99**
- ☐ Golden, 95, **99**
- ☐ Egret, Great, **89**
- ☐ Snowy, **89**
- ☐ Falcon, Peregrine, **117**
- ☐ Prairie, **117**
- ☐ Finch, Cassin's, **401**, 403
- ☐ House, clb, 401, **403**, 407
- ☐ Purple, **401**, 403
- ☐ Flicker, Northern, clb, 211, **221**

☐ Flycatcher, Ash-throated, **235**, 237
☐ Cordilleran, **227**
☐ Dusky, 227, 229, **231**
☐ Gray, **231**
☐ Hammond's, 227, **229**, 231
☐ Olive-sided, **225**
☐ Pacific-slope, **227**
☐ Willow, 225, **227**
☐ Gadwall, 29, **31**
☐ Gnatcatcher, Blue-gray, **279**
☐ Godwit, Marbled, 137, **145**
☐ Goldeneye, Barrow's, **49**
☐ Common, 47, **49**
☐ Goldfinch, American, clb, 381, **409**, 411
☐ Lesser, 381, **409**
☐ Goose, Canada, clb, 19, **23**
☐ Cackling, **23**
☐ Greater White-fronted, **19**, 23
☐ Ross's, **21**
☐ Snow, **21**, 25, 81
☐ Goshawk, Northern, 103, **105**
☐ Grackle, Common, **391**
☐ Grebe, Clark's, **79**
☐ Eared, 73, 75, **77**
☐ Horned, 73, **75**, 77, 79
☐ Pied-billed, **73**, 121
☐ Red-necked, **75**
☐ Western, 75, **79**
☐ Grosbeak, Black-headed, **379**, 395, 411
☐ Evening, **411**
☐ Pine, **399**, 405

☐ Grouse, Dusky, 61, **65**
☐ Greater Sage-, 59, **63**
☐ Ruffed, **61**, 65
☐ Sharp-tailed, 59, **63**
☐ Spruce, 61, **65**
☐ Gull, Bonaparte's, **153**
☐ California, **155**, 157
☐ Franklin, **153**
☐ Glaucous-winged, **159**
☐ Herring, **157**, 159
☐ Ring-billed, **155**
☐ Harrier, Northern, **101**, 191
☐ Hawk, Cooper's, 101, **103**, 105
☐ Ferruginous, 109, **111**
☐ Red-tailed, clb, 107, **109**, 111, 113
☐ Rough-legged, **113**
☐ Sharp-shinned, **103**, 115
☐ Swainson's, **107**, 109
☐ Heron, Great Blue, clb, **87**, 123
☐ Hummingbird, Anna's, **201**, 203, 205
☐ Black-chinned, **201**, 203
☐ Broad-tailed, 203, **205**
☐ Calliope, **203**, 205
☐ Rufous, 203, **205**
☐ Ibis, White-faced, **93**
☐ Jay, Blue, **247**
☐ Gray, **245**, 253
☐ Pinyon, 249, **251**
☐ Steller's, **247**, 249
☐ Western Scrub-, 247, **249**, 251

☐ Junco, Dark-eyed, clb, 349, **375**
☐ Kestrel, American, clb, **115**
☐ Killdeer, clb, **127**
☐ Kingbird, Eastern, **237**
☐ Western, clb, 235, **237**
☐ Kingfisher, Belted, **207**
☐ Kinglet, Golden-crowned, **299**
☐ Ruby-crowned, **299**
☐ Lark, Horned, **261**, 321, 377
☐ Longspur, Lapland, 261, 357, **377**
☐ Loon, Common, **71**, 83
☐ Pacific, **71**
☐ Magpie, Black-billed, clb, **255**
☐ Mallard, clb, **31**
☐ Meadowlark, Western, clb, **387**
☐ Merganser, Common, **53**
☐ Hooded, 27, **51**
☐ Red-breasted, **53**
☐ Merlin, **115**
☐ Nighthawk, Common, clb, **195**
☐ Night-Heron, Black-crowned, 85, **91**
☐ Nutcracker, Clark's, 245, **253**, 255
☐ Nuthatch, Pygmy, 281, 283, **285**
☐ Red-breasted, **281**, 283, 285
☐ White-breasted, 281, **283**, 285
☐ Oriole, Bullock's, clb, **347**, 395

☐ Osprey, **97**
☐ Owl, Barn, **171**, 179
☐ Barred, **185**, 187
☐ Burrowing, **183**
☐ Flammulated, **173**, 175
☐ Great Gray, 185, **187**
☐ Great Horned, **177**, 189
☐ Long-eared, 177, **189**, 191
☐ Northern Pygmy-, **181**, 193
☐ Northern Saw-whet, 175, 181, **193**
☐ Short-eared, 101, 171, 183, 189, **191**
☐ Snowy, 171, **179**
☐ Western Screech, 173, **175**, 181, 193
☐ Partridge, Gray, **57**
☐ Pelican, American White, **81**
☐ Phalarope, Red-necked, 149, **151**
☐ Wilson's, **149**, 151
☐ Pheasant, Ring-necked, **59**
☐ Phoebe, Say's, **233**
☐ Pigeon, Rock, clb, **167**
☐ Pintail, Northern, **37**
☐ Pipit, American, 261, **321**
☐ Plover, Black-bellied, **125**
☐ Semipalmated, **127**
☐ Poorwill, Common, **195**
☐ Pygmy-Owl, Northern, **181**, 193
☐ Quail, California, clb, **69**
☐ Mountain, 57, **69**
☐ Rail, Virginia, **119**
☐ Raven, Common, clb, 257, **259**

- Redhead, 37, **41**
- Redpoll, Common, **407**
- Redstart, American, **337**
- Robin, American, clb, **311**, 313, 379
- Rosy-Finch, Black, **397**
  - Gray-crowned, **397**
- Sage-Grouse, Greater, 59, **63**
- Sandpiper, Baird's, **141**, 143
  - Least, **139**, 141
  - Pectoral, **141**
  - Spotted, **135**
  - Western, **139**, 141, 143
- Sapsucker, Red-breasted, **213**
  - Red-naped, **213**
  - Williamson's, **211**, 213, 221
- Scaup, Greater, 41, 43, **45**
  - Lesser, 41, 43, **45**
- Screech-Owl, Western, 173, **175**, 181, 193
- Scrub-Jay, Western, 247, **249**, 251
- Shoveler, Northern, 31, 33, **35**
- Shrike, Northern, **239**
  - Loggerhead, **239**
- Siskin, Pine, 405, **407**
- Snipe, Wilson's, **147**
- Solitaire, Townsend's, **303**
- Sora, **119**
- Sparrow, American Tree, **351**, 353
  - Black-throated, **361**
  - Brewer's, 353, **355**
  - Chipping, 351, **353**, 355, 359

- Fox, **365**, 367
- Golden-crowned, 371, **373**
- Grasshopper, **363**
- Harris's, **373**
- House, clb, **413**
- Lark, **359**
- Lincoln's, 367, **369**
- Sage, **361**
- Savannah, 357, **363**, 367
- Song, 365, **367**, 369
- Vesper, **357**, 359, 375
- White-crowned, clb, **371**, 373
- White-throated, **371**, 373
- Starling, European, clb, **319**, 323, 391
- Stilt, Black-necked, **129**
- Swallow, Barn, clb, 271, **273**
  - Bank, 263, 267, **269**
  - Cliff, clb, **271**, 273
  - Northern Rough-winged, 263, **267**, 269
  - Tree, **263**, 265, 267, 269
  - Violet-green, 199, 263, **265**
- Swan, Trumpeter, **25**
  - Tundra, **25**
- Swift, Vaux's, **197**
  - White-throated, 197, **199**
- Tanager, Western, **347**, 395
- Teal, Blue-winged, **33**, 39
  - Cinnamon, 29, **33**, 39
  - Green-winged, 33, **39**
- Tern, Black, **165**
  - Caspian, **161**, 163
  - Common, **163**

☐ Forster's, **163**
☐ Thrasher, Sage, **317**
☐ Thrush, Hermit, 305, 307, **309**
☐ Swainson's, 305, **307**, 309
☐ Varied, 311, **313**
☐ Titmouse, Juniper, **275**, 279
☐ Towhee, Green-tailed, **349**
☐ Spotted, **349**
☐ Turkey, Wild, **67**
☐ Veery, **305**, 307, 309
☐ Vireo, Cassin's, **241**, 243
☐ Plumbeous, **241**
☐ Red-eyed, **243**, 401
☐ Warbling, **243**, 401
☐ Vulture, Turkey, **95**, 99
☐ Warbler, Black-throated Gray, **333**, 335
☐ MacGillivray's, 327, **339**, 341
☐ Nashville, **327**, 339, 341
☐ Orange-crowned, **325**, 329, 339, 341, 343
☐ Townsend's, 333, **335**
☐ Virginia's, **327**
☐ Wilson's, 329, **343**
☐ Yellow, 325, **329**, 341, 343
☐ Yellow-rumped, **331**
☐ Waxwing, Bohemian, **323**
☐ Cedar, clb, **323**
☐ Wigeon, American, **29**, 31
☐ Eurasian, **29**
☐ Willet, **133**
☐ Woodpecker, American Three-toed, 215, **219**
☐ Black-backed, 209, **219**

☐ Downy, **215**, 219
☐ Hairy, **215**, 219
☐ Lewis's, **209**
☐ Pileated, **223**
☐ White-headed, **217**
☐ Wood-Pewee, Western, **225**
☐ Wren, Bewick's, 289, **291**, 295
☐ Canyon, **289**
☐ House, clb, 289, **291**, 293, 295,
☐ Marsh, 291, **295**
☐ Rock, **289**
☐ Winter, 291, **293**
☐ Yellowlegs, Greater, **131**, 133
☐ Lesser, **131**, 149
☐ Yellowthroat, Common, **341**, 345

Other Species Seen

_____

_____

_____

_____

_____

_____

_____

About the Authors

Mike Denny

Born in Klamath Falls, Oregon, Mike took up birding at eight while living in southeastern Africa where he was in awe of all things living. Returning to the US, he studied Biology, met his wife MerryLynn, and now lives to bird in the Walla Walla Valley of Washington.

Dave Trochlell

Idaho and Western Montana regional editor for *North American Birds* since 1997, member of the Idaho Bird Records Committee, former editor for the Idaho Christmas Bird Counts, author and editor for various birding and natural resources publications.

Harry Nehls

Has birded extensively in Eastern Oregon since 1949. He lectures and writes about birds for the Audubon Society of Portland, has authored three books, and serves as Secretary of the Oregon Record Committee and subregional editor for *North American Birds*.